Ready, Plan, Homeschool!
Effective Scheduling for Homeschooling Families

Purva Brown

TABLE OF CONTENTS

How to Use This Book	7
First Stop	11
Templates	43
Time Management Strategies	69
Subjects	103
Challenges & Questions	123
Acknowledgments	161

HOW TO USE THIS BOOK

This book is a quick and dirty manual for jumping into homeschooling. If you've considered it for a while, but are unsure, needing a little inspiration on scheduling your days, or otherwise wanting to hear what's working and what's not from a type B mom in the trenches, this book is for you.

I have divided the book into three chunks. It is not necessary to read it beginning to end to get the most out of it. Feel free to jump around and read whatever strikes you.

First Stop offers a general philosophy of homeschooling. If you already read my blog or have read my other books, you could skip this section and move straight into the next.

The real meat of the book is in the middle. *Templates* considers how to think about a schedule when it comes to homeschooling. In *Time Management Strategies*, I discuss what has and has not worked for us as a homeschooling family. It talks about how I like to structure our day, drawing inspiration from books, friends and, to be perfectly honest, bad days. Under *Subjects*, I write about how we deal with specific subjects in our homeschool.

The last section in the book deals with challenges and issues that you may or may not face while homeschooling and how to deal with them.

Happy homeschooling! I'd love to hear your feedback at threedegreesfromperfect@gmail.com

FIRST STOP

Math word problems have long been the bane of my existence. I find the way they are taught in various curricula to be despicable. Often, children are taught to look for cue words like "difference" or "total" instead of understanding what the problem is about and what it is really asking.

There is a reason for this, of course. It's because word problems require logical thinking instead of grammatical thinking. If you've read my book *The Classical Unschooler*, you know that even though we are mostly unschoolers, I tend to take the classical model of learning quite seriously. In a nutshell, the classical theory of education says is that learning proceeds from grammar to logic to rhetoric with no short cuts.

For me then, makes sense then to set aside word problems until the children are ready to get to the logic stage and focus on basic arithmetic in the grammar stage. I find that it makes no sense to try and solve word problems with a first grader who is just learning to read and do basic addition and subtraction.

As I write this book, however, my older two children are well on their way into the last year of what would be considered elementary grade levels in math. And so now that they're older, we're back to solving word problems. They're still not our favorite thing on the menu, however.

We were discussing this at dinner the other day.

I was recounting our day to my husband and I mentioned how word problems are, well, a problem, because more often than not, the children want to rush to the answer immediately. This isn't always possible because there is more than one step involved in finding the answer.

"If you would just not freak out, calm down, read the question carefully, it would all make sense," I suggested, perhaps for the umpteenth time.

My daughter looked guilty.

And then my husband said something with uncommonly good sense, which is why I love him and we've been married so many years.

He said, "You think it's about finding out the answer, but really, the first step is not about finding the answer, it's about figuring out the question."

Brilliant, right? And so very important on so many levels, especially when it comes to scheduling your day when it comes to homeschooling your children.

What is your question? What is it you are really setting out to do? What is your end goal? Do you have one in mind? Is it realistic? Can you name and define it?

These are good things to ask yourself when homeschooling. What is your question? Why are you doing this? What do you hope to achieve? What is the unique perspective you bring to the situation? What are your limitations? And what are your strengths? Don't ignore these questions. They might be nagging doubts right now simmering under the surface.

Expose them and truly get ready to drill down into them.

Asking the right questions can help you calm down and focus; they will help you not run in ten directions all at once. They will also enhance the possibility that you will actually find the right answers instead of trying to guess at ten others.

So, before you begin your homeschool schedule, before you begin a new curriculum, before you begin your day, ask yourself, "What is the question?"

Tony Robbins in *Awaken The Giant Within* says that when he interviewed successful people, the biggest difference he noticed between them and the people who had been unable to find success (in any field, mind you) was that that former asked better questions and as a result, got better answers.

Not only is it important to ask better questions – of yourself, of your family and of your children, it is also imperative to be able to become aware of the ones you might be answering unconsciously. When scheduling a homeschooling day, this could mean that you need to be brutally honest with yourself about your goals and ends.

For instance, are you penciling something into your schedule because you're feeling pressured into doing something you don't think is truly important? Is it peer pressure to conform to an idea of a certain kind of homeschooler? Are you imitating someone whose style appeals to you? Are you hopelessly stretched? Or are you truly able to see what your children need, what you need and are willing to work hard to make time for all of that?

What is the question? Or the questions, for that matter? Think about those first. Get a sheet of paper and just start writing them down. Don't rush to answer them. Just sit with the questions for a while. Ask some good ones. Then ask some that are better.

*

So here's a good question: what's the easiest way to get frustrated as a homeschooler? Answer: trying to fit into a mold that is clearly not made for you or for your kids.

There are a few ways this can happen. Let's talk of the most common ones. In my experience, these mistakes happen most often around the first or second year of homeschooling. Usually, parents who persist beyond the third year of homeschooling figure things out and settle into some basic patterns comfortable to them.

The most common way I see people get frustrated as homeschoolers right off the bat is by trying to fit into an education philosophy they don't really believe.

Let's consider this one: organization. If I had a dollar for every time someone says they can't homeschool because they're not organized, I'd be rich beyond my dreams. Here's the thing, though. That thing about being organized? Not every homeschooler is organized! I write about this often enough that if you're a reader of my blog, you've come across a few posts about it. I am still constantly surprised, though, at the number of people who tell me that they can't homeschool because they're not organized.

Here's what has (maybe) happened: somewhere along the line, these people met a homeschooler who liked being organized. That was the specific personality and perhaps, philosophy of education this homeschooler adhered to. But it is by no means the only way to get it done! So if you adopt the idea that you must be organized and buckle down and grit your teeth for the first few weeks, color coding and taking attendance and filing schoolwork, but then run out of will power and want to throw your kids in the first school bus that comes along, chances are you've got the wrong idea of how homeschooling is supposed to look for you and your family.

Education does not happen because the children are ready at nine a.m., hair combed and teeth brushed, pencils sharpened. It does not happen because you they can obey you or listen for your voice or their name (Ugh, I can't tell you how many times I felt inadequate as a mom because my children didn't hear me, didn't listen or interrupted me while I was talking to someone!) in a crowded room. They are not educated because they have manners.

While these contribute to refinement and ease things in terms of interpersonal relationships, education can and often does happen outside of these trappings. There are plenty of good families who have wonderful relationships and fantastic educations who struggle to appear "well-behaved" by definition. Chances are, they asked the right questions or came around to them eventually.

Figure out your family's characteristics, your own personality, your child's personality and work with it. Don't force homeschooling in a top down manner and then get discouraged.

*

Closely related to organization is buying the wrong curriculum. We live in the golden age of homeschooling. It's mainstream, almost no one asks about socialization any more and heck, even Elon Musk says he's unschooling his child. Cool, right?

Well, not so fast. Here's the problem.

There are homeschooling workshops everywhere you look. There are countless numbers of books about how to do it right. Curricula now fills the first ten pages of a simple Google search. For a new homeschooling family, overwhelment can quickly take the place of excitement.

Welcome to the golden age of homeschooling where we now have a tyranny of choice. What curriculum will you choose? Which book will you read? What classes will your child take? What is your style of teaching? How about the style of your child? Which books will you pick?

Sigh. Even as I write this, I know. I have my own contributions to this. Recently someone on my Facebook page posted that she didn't have the resources we did when it came to homeschooling her kids and isn't it wonderful that we do?

Yes, yes, yes, I agree. However…

Now, don't get me wrong. I am definitely *not* bemoaning having choices, simply stating that they can get overwhelming very quickly. I love being about to ask questions in Facebook groups, to look something up, to buy a new curriculum (or no curriculum for that matter!) if one goes sour.

But all these choices can sometimes be paralyzing and downright frustrating. Faced with a hundred options, some will curriculum-hop, others will delay choosing at all, while some others will try to cram it all in.

Please don't do that! If you can, avoid all those extremes. So what's the way out of this? The way out is the way in. Even before you begin, ask better questions.

If this is your first year of homeschooling – and especially if this is your first year – don't begin with searching for curricula of any kind. Spend more time dreaming. Yes, you read that right. I said *dreaming*. Day-dreaming, rather.

Spend some time creating mental maps of what you want your homeschooling and your family to look like during this time. Then work backwards from there. It's called beginning with the end in mind and it works very well.

Beginning with the end in mind works because it eliminates some options. Spend some time removing things before adding them and you'll notice that choosing (and planning!) gets easier.

Of course, the most common way to get frustrated as a new homeschooler is by listening to the wrong experts or to too many of them. This one is the hardest hurdle to avoid because it is sometimes difficult to come to a conviction about homeschooling without reading books by the greats. So much has been written about education and there are so many fantastic writers and thinkers out there, that I am loathe to tell you not to read them.

Take Gatto and Holt, for example. It's rare to come across an unschooler who hasn't read their work. I was in fact introduced to them by an unschooling mom who noticed I was checking out books on homeschooling from our local library.

What I read resonated with me. However, unlike many radical unschoolers, I also liked the classical model of learning and I do put some stock into memorizing things instead of simply looking them up. So my affiliation with either group – classical and unschooling – was a little off.

You might find yourself in a similar boat. And when that happens, you have to tell yourself that you are free. As a homeschooler, choosing an affiliation can be tricky.

At any point, if what the person/friend/blogger/expert/teacher says (and yes, I include myself here) you are free to disagree to him or her and do things your way. Yes, this counts even if the person is dead. (I'm looking at you, Mason and Montessori.)

Who cares if that's not the way to establish a good habit? Who cares if that's how children were taught in Ancient and Medieval times? If it doesn't work for your family, do it the way it works. Period.

You're in this for your children, not for anyone else. Choose an education for them before you choose an affiliation for yourself. It will be less frustrating all in all and will provide a good starting point for asking the right questions.

*

What is your biggest reason to homeschool? I'll tell you mine. Right from the start, it was about conversations. My daughter didn't speak until she was four. No, I'm not lying. But when she did, we began to have the most fascinating conversations and when the youngest baby came along, well, we discovered what most homeschoolers realize: we're in it for the long haul because we love the time we spend together.

The best thing about homeschooling is the unique perspective I get from my children and what I'm able to give them. Homeschooling for our family is nothing without conversations.

Consider this. We were riding along one day headed to the grocery store when my son, then four or five, piped up from the back of our minivan:

"Mom, money comes from the President."

"No, that's not true," I replied. "Can you think of how money is created?"

"In the mint?"

We had a fairly long talk about money and value and how it's created after that.

After all, one of the things we try to do often is to connect money, value and work for the children from a very young age. It is the reason we pay them for chores and make sure they can spend it in small ways they wish every week.

I knew the conversation wouldn't be the last.

We leave room in our homeschool planning for conversation. Part of our car schooling strategy is to get out of the house once a week. When we are in the car, all we do is memorize with CDs and such. And then, we leave a chunk of time – a nice, blank slate – for conversations.

Some days, nothing happens. But quite often, the most interesting questions come up.

"If the President changes, do all the laws change?"

"What are taxes?"

"How much money do we have?"

"What is a budget?"

"What if we could use grass as money?"

"If we make something and sell it, the cheaper we make it, the more people buy it, right? That's the way to make a lot of money."

Of course, economics, politics and civics are not the only conversations we have in the car but I am surprised by how often even the littlest children do think about such things. These are the very things people seem to relegate to a much later age for teaching and I've often wondered why.

While I'm not a fan of preschool and early education, I absolutely think that even elementary aged kids can and should be taught basic economics, history and civics. Of course, if we tend to see these skills as subjects per se, we tend to push them forward because, well, the children need to understand what money is to begin with and then percentages and interest and this and that *before* we get into it, right?

Nope. Wrong.

All they need to understand is that money isn't the note or the coin. Money is value. It is only in conversations that you can make that connection and then build on it.

Let me give you another example.

I had a friend in graduate school who used to irritate me by asking the professor one too many questions. Usually, the questions were of an open-ended sort.

"Doesn't this seem a little fatalistic?" she asked of Yeats' *The Second Coming*, for example. This grated on my nerves.

"Why do you ask so many questions?" I said. Me, classroom-hater, classroom fanatic. Part of me wanted the lesson over with and part of me just wanted to read the poem and let it sink in. I didn't want to discuss it and, in my opinion, dissect it to death.

"Because I've always believed," she responded, "that education is a two-way street."

We tend to forget that when it comes to educating children, I think. In spite of the constant reminders through memes about educating literally meaning "to draw out," we tend to sometimes think that just dumping a bunch of information into kids and then seeing how quickly they can regurgitate those facts is somehow teaching them.

I remember being terrified of teaching my own children when we first began to think of homeschooling. Perhaps it was because I tend to be an introvert and the idea of standing in front of a group and teaching them seemed, frankly, intimidating.

It wasn't until I realized that homeschooling isn't like teaching a classroom – you don't have to work hard to get and keep their attention, it really doesn't take very long at all and it provides you with ample opportunities for your own intellectual stimulation and perhaps a side profession.

Homeschooling is intimate in the way a performance on a stage is not. One of the biggest advantages homeschooling has over a classroom setting is that it is intimate. Like a conversation, it is a shared experience between the teacher and the student, a mother and her child, a father and his son or daughter. There is time to ask questions and have them answered. There is time to read a story, explore the segues, learn something as an accident.

Homeschooling often is learning just by the way, as a side effect, just for the heck of it, just because it is so darn fun! None of this is possible in a classroom or in a performance.

Homeschooling can also be very individualized. My son for example moved on to multiplication while my daughter needed more practice with subtraction, so I kept her there. The thing is this: she's older than him. This is not a big deal with us because I don't stress about their grade levels.

In a classroom where they would be expected to be in lock step with their peers, this would be a problem. But in a home setting, who cares? They're learning to mastery, they're learning to their interests and I'm giving them free rein where they want it and where they excel.

The same daughter who needs more practice in subtraction is reading way above her grade level. She has practical skills unmatched in children her age. She is creative, curious and incredibly smart. She sketches, draws and creates comic strips. Individualized education serves her well.

My favorite thing about homeschooling, though, is that it can be made to be introspective. In today's world information is everywhere. There is very little stays that hidden for very long. I can learn anything I want at the tap of a few keystrokes.

But it's not gathering information that counts as education, I don't think. It's learning how to process it.

Where's the time to process anything in a classroom that does not end as an uncomfortable consensus between the quiet ones and those who are extroverted? Where's the time to even think? I'm reminded of this often when I ask my son a question and his eyes glaze over and when I push him, he says, "I'm trying to think!" He really is. But this wouldn't fly in a classroom.

Susan Cain in *Quiet* says that by its nature, education favors the extroverted child because you're putting everyone in a high stimulation setting. She admits the best way to educate is one on one.

Even if your children are extroverts, we do them a disservice by putting them in high stimulation environments all the time. One of the tenets of our homeschool is giving the children enough time to be bored, to make their own fun. Homeschooling gives them time to think, to process, to introspect. There is down time to piece together what they learned in the day, ask good questions and we even have time to find good answers.

As a homeschooler, I never have to worry about giving a good performance. I only have to engage enough to have a great conversation. Because that's what teaching really is. And that's what will always remain the enduring beauty of home education.

If the curriculum you choose doesn't leave room for meaningful conversations with your children and replaces it instead with classroom-like adherence to a system, or worse, intends to hire you or your children as performers in it, ditch it immediately.

*

"Wait!" you say. "Did you just say to ditch a curriculum?" Gasp.

One of the biggest questions anyone who is considering homeschooling gets is about curriculum.

"Where will you buy the material to teach them with?" I was asked when I first started.

I shrugged my shoulders. It wasn't something I was even remotely concerned about, but some of the older moms who had maybe considered homeschooling their now adult children remembered.

There was a time when curriculum was hard to find. I know it sounds crazy today, but there was a time when publishers would not sell curriculum to parents, only to schools. There was a time when homeschooling was illegal. I have heard firsthand accounts and met some of these people who put together their own curriculum, used the Bible and other available resources, including letters which arrived in the mail, to teach their children.

We are living in the best of times.

But the time comes with its own downfalls. We have too much. Ask any homeschooler what curriculum they're using and you'll know they're bombarded. Google "homeschool curriculum" and you'll see what I mean.

In this overbombardment, it is hard to keep it simple.

In fact, I think it is the very ubiquity of curricula that makes everyone want to replicate school at home. The very thing that made parents rebel against public schools, wanting to teach their own children, do things the way their families did them, give children a broader world than schools can ever offer, it is that very thing that now encourages parents to fall back into the old trap, that old box that they fought so hard to break.

But one of the biggest things you learn when you begin homeschooling is that time spent with a book in front of you does not equal learning. You can spend all day at a desk and come away knowing as little as when you started.

As an article in *Business Insider* explains, the 10,000-hour rule made famous by author Malcolm Gladwell only works for certain domains. These domains have stable structures like classical music and chess. It accounts for less than 4% of a difference in education and a mere 1% in the professional domain. One percent! Think about that.

And even then, that 10,000-hour rule refers to deliberate practice which sitting at a desk passively is definitely *not*.

If you want to learn more about deliberate practice, I recommend reading *Talent is Overrated* by Geoff Colvin.

Focus on education, not time. This concern with time is especially important for homeschoolers and unschoolers. When I recently wrote that we begin our school year in January, a reader expressed concern that it might throw off the date of graduation.

While it is normal to worry about this, especially in states where you are required to show a certain number of hours for "school," I think the concern is unnecessary. It might even be misleading.

You do not need to worry about time spent in front of a textbook; you only need to think about if the lesson was learned. (This is another reason I don't like using a box curriculum. Most boxed curricula come with schedules.)

Better yet to focus on the process that was undertaken to understand the lesson. SATs and ACTs - if your child is headed to college at all - focus not so much on the material, but on the ability to process information and glean meaning out of it.

Don't worry about hours spent at a desk. Spend time in conversation. Choose to teach what matters to you and hones your child's talents.

Hours and minutes do not equal an education - the ability to learn does. As long as you have imparted the how of learning, you do not need to concern yourself with the what.

And the how takes far less time than you would imagine.

*

Let's ask the question this way: what do you think are your greatest assets? If I stopped you in the street knowing that you were planning on starting homeschooling, what would you say are your family's biggest assets *right now?*

They're not your books. And neither are they your learning styles. And, sorry to say, no matter how much you love them, it's not your children or your children's friends.

As a homeschooling family, you have two assets: time and liberty. And don't you forget it.

Let's talk first about time.

I will admit I love planning more than most people. I love playing around with schedules and seeing what works. My children have done their sit-down work at night, in the evenings, first thing in the mornings, and I am open to them all.

As a homeschooler, you're not wasting time. You're not taking attendance or spending as much time disciplining. Since most of your time is spent directly involved in face to face work with your children, you have more time.

And it's not just you. I know it's easy to forget that when all your social media posts emphasize how happy the parents are that the kids are back in school in the fall, but remember that your kids actually have more time to pursue what they want as homeschoolers.

As the old song goes, time actually is on your side.

Closely related to time is, of course, liberty. The freedom you have in homeschooling, I think, is not taken seriously enough because we are sometimes so focused on grade levels and keeping children in lockstep with their public schooled peers.

I know I do. I always have an eye to academics and I do worry about grade levels, even when I try not to.

But here's the thing. Even with that concern, even with dedicated time set aside to work diligently on math, reading and writing, homeschooling families have huge chunks of time! We can work on what pleases us, makes us come alive.

It is easy for a homeschooling family to forget this. It is easy to appoint a public or charter school over ourselves, to trade this freedom for some supposed reward. Of course, this is every individual family's decision, but think hard and long before you decide to do so.

Time and freedom are your biggest assets. Don't treat them lightly.

*

If time and freedom are our biggest assets and we want to work in accordance with that idea, it must follow that we don't want to fritter them away just to keep curriculum makers and other classroom-at-home-types happy.

So, when it comes to homeschooling, our family takes a very practical stance. My daughter has taken to asking, "But when will I ever use this in real life?" And if between my husband and me we cannot come up with a good answer, we usually ditch the specific topic and move on.

This might seem overly confident and even brazen (or scary!) to some people, but if you think about it, it makes perfect sense.

What did you learn in school that you use today? And the corollary, how much more did you learn after being done with your so-called education?

Perhaps an example would help clarify what I'm talking about.

After much hemming and hawing, we have started to use an online curriculum mainly for math and spelling practice. I didn't bother to do this at younger ages (as I mention in my book *The Classical Unschooler* I don't teach word problems until after third grade) because we simply focused on memorizing tables and doing basic calculations.

When the older two (my youngest is six) outgrew basic math and needed more practice, we started to use IXL, which adjusts its difficulty levels to the children's abilities.

However, we feel no pressure to complete every last unit. Let's face it. I'm too much of an unschooler to do that.

We recently came across some fractions (Yes, I did the basics of adding and subtracting and multiplying and dividing fractions, before anyone feels the need to tell me that the concept is important. I get it.) that I didn't see the children ever – and I do mean ever using. Ever. Because, really, 67ths of something? What are we, Babylon? So I felt free to dump them. And I did. But not before mentioning it on my Facebook page.

And that was (maybe) where I messed up.

People came out of the woodwork to tell me how important fractions are because – get this – if the children ever get into woodworking. (Haha… get it? People coming out of the woodwork? See what I did there?)

I can assure you, if my kids want to learn woodworking, they can learn their 67ths then. I refuse to teach something as a "just in case" when they're not interested in it and it's flipping hard.

Unfortunately, that's the rationale for a lot of what they're expected to learn. Here. Learn some trigonometry. It will come in handy. Just in case. And yes, you must know how to diagram sentences, in case those barbarians from the Middle Ages show up and want to add words to our dictionary.

Oh, wait.

Well, I refuse.

I refuse to teach things that don't immediately impress their relevance upon me. Because here's the thing: we don't know how the future is going to look. We have no idea the kind of jobs the kids are going to have. (And I doubt it's going to be woodworking.)

My job as a homeschooler is not to cram every last thing just in case into my children's heads, because let's face it, that never works. My job is to give them the tools to learn what they will need to in the future. Forcing them to learn something they hate is the very opposite of what I'm trying to do in our homeschool.

"Just in case" is not a rationale for learning useless information and skills. Especially when those skills are difficult. Stop using it.

*

I recently read *Essentialism – The Disciplined Pursuit of Less* by Greg McKeown. I devoured it whole in one sitting last evening.

Even though it is a business book, I think our current culture of supposed harried moms who eat this concoction we refer to as "mom guilt" would benefit immensely from reading it.

Take for example this nugget I found.

"An editor is not someone who merely says no to things. A three year old can do that. Nor does an editor simply eliminate; in a way, an editor actually adds. […] a good editor uses deliberate subtraction to actually add life. […] Likewise, in life, disciplined editing can increase your ability to focus on and give energy to the things that really matter."

I might be an editor at heart.

I find that moms who know their number one priority on any given day seem happier in general and are less likely to say they suffer mom guilt.

So how do you avoid mom guilt? Here are some suggestions.

Discern what's really important

McKeown suggests setting aside some time to discern what's most important. As moms, we are bombarded with decisions every minute and they all can seem vital. Add to that the pressures of social media and each day seems to evaporate before it even begins.

As I mentioned at the beginning of this section, set some time aside periodically to think, not just about the daily or weekly to-do and grocery shopping list, but the bigger picture. What are you trying to achieve? What do you want to teach your children? How do you want your home to look?

Be realistic. Be concrete and then ruthlessly eliminate everything else that takes away from those goals. And suffer no mom guilt for it. Mom guilt stems mostly from feeling like you should do something when you have no desire or inclination to do so. It is a result of letting others decide for you.

It is easier to eliminate mom guilt if you have consciously chosen one thing over another.

Also, don't downplay the tradeoffs. Tradeoffs are inevitable because we're human and we cannot do everything. But I don't think we realize that. As moms, we think we must do everything and do it right away. Not true.

When my husband and I decided to homeschool, I knew there were certain things we were going to have to give up – things like me having a job outside the home, or being able to go places during the day without children.

When we decided to unschool, there were certain assurances we were sacrificing – things like whether the kids would in lock-step academically with their public schooled peers. When we decided to save money to pay off the mortgage, to never be in debt, there were consequences to that – the budget had to be maintained, there were no long vacations, we had to live frugally and make the most of it.

Everything has a trade-off. If you haven't taken the time to think through these things, guilt will likely follow and you will be right back running from one form of mom guilt to another.

Hang on tight!

Choice, says McKeown, is not a thing, it's an *action*.

We don't have choice, we *choose*. But there is an art to choosing. His criterion is that if something isn't an absolute yes, then it's an absolute no. (He says that if your reaction to anything is not a "Hell, yeah!" you should go with "No.") Tough, but effective.

Thought about this way, every decision is put into perspective against your (limited) time, your (short) life. I think mom guilt assumes we have more than twenty-four hours in a day, that we have no need for sleep, that we have unlimited room in our tired bedheads, and no need for any other human contact but the kids. All are fallacies.

When you choose, hang on tight; chances are you will be required to continue choosing the thing you have chosen.

Which brings us right back to the quote about editing above. Moms without mom guilt are great editors.

When I taught my kids subtraction, it was amusing to see how nervous it made them to take things away. Even though they were good at it, they wanted to jump straight to multiplication.

But we stayed there a while, subtracting, removing, eliminating. It was the best thing we learned all year.

*

We're getting really close to the part of the book where I talk about the specifics of templates and scheduling, but before that, I have to mention one small thing. There's a reason moms in general and homeschooling moms in particular tend to waste time. Want to know the secret? Here it is.

Boredom.

Yes, I said it. And before you throw a brick at me, let me start with saying that I'm speaking from personal experience. The real reason I don't manage time well is that old b word.

Boredom grabs a hold of me as soon as I open my eyes in the morning. It's the real reason I want to grab the covers, pull them back over my head and go back to sleep.

I'm bored. What have I look forward to after all? Getting the baby's diaper changed? Making breakfast, lunch and dinner? Going over 2 + 3 drills? Sounding out h-a-t one more time? Yawn. Let's go to bed already.

In my desire to give my children a good upbringing while managing money wisely, I am often bored. And because I'm bored, I squander time.

I mean, why should I care about how productive I can be in doing dishes or meal planning for twenty minutes if the rest of the day stretches intolerably long in front of me with never-ending squabbles between siblings? Who cares how quickly I can get done with school if there's nothing else to do but make dinner, clean up and plan it again for tomorrow in an endless loop? Isn't Facebook drama then way more exciting?

But wait. Here's the thing. Once I realized boredom was the real reason for my lack of desire to manage my time well, it was relatively easy to fix.

So today think about this: what can you do (besides get embroiled in drama of the social media and/or streaming kind) that will make your life less boring without spending tons of money? What are your passions that you have supposedly set aside after having children?

I'll tell you mine. I love learning. I have a few pet obsessions, if you will, that I cycle through on a pretty regular basis: history, finance, teaching, theology, weight lifting, planning, organizing, business, psychology. I'm pretty sure I'm forgetting something.

However, I find that I can usually find something to work on every day that grabs my interest in this pile. And the sooner I get done with my usual routine, the more time I have to devote to these. And in today's internet age, you can learn anything you want online. Podcasts, internet radio, books, blogs, e-readers, streaming videos – frankly, it's an exciting time to learn!

Some of my friends like to make things and if you're crafty, it's even more important to manage your time better to get that big chunk of time to make something, to build, to create.

There is beauty all around you. There isn't enough time to be bored. I'm guessing you've probably said this to your children. Now say it to yourself and take it to heart.

TEMPLATES

Now that you are inspired and ready to homeschool and hopefully know a little about what kind of homeschooler you are, it's time to think about The Schedule.

How will you organize your days? What will they look like? Where do you envision getting the hard work of educating your children done? How would you ideally like to get it done? Do you see yourself outdoors? Or do you see yourself reading on the couch? Or at the dining table? How many hours will you dedicate to it? Will it be mostly on weekday mornings as is most common or do you intend to get the bulk of work done on evenings and weekends?

Seem overwhelming to decide all that *right this minute?* It doesn't have to be. Let me introduce you to the power of the template.

A few years ago, I gave up drinking coffee. (Don't gasp. I'm back to it now. It was a good experiment.) The caffeine was interfering with my ability to think and leaving me feeling worn out and jittery, so I decided I would be better off without it for a while.

The results were immediate. I distinctly remember feeling like I carried around my personal fog with me. Everything seemed gray. The feeling was accentuated by the rainy days we were experiencing. All I wanted was sleep. In fact, I sat down at one point only to wake up an hour later. I had in fact fallen asleep without meaning to!

The good news, however, was this: I discovered that the only thing that went off without a hitch was our homeschool day. Homeschooling was not hard!

Sometimes when you mention a *schedule*, people balk. I do, too. If you plunked down a few tasks in front of me and said, "Okay, so do these in the same order every single day until you don't have to think about them!" I probably won't know where to start.

So don't start – yet. The trick is to figure out the template before you start.

Think about it. The weather has a template – summer, fall, winter and spring follow with regularity. Night follows day. Recessions follow expansions. What are these but templates?

Figure out your rhythm, your template for homeschooling before you create a schedule and you will do far better.

How do you do this? Take a good look at your day. Don't think of the ideal day, think of a normal day. Don't try to change it or idealize it. Simply observe it and note it down.

Then figure out what you can include in your day or how you can arrange it to fit you and your family best. If you don't like working out first thing in the morning, don't! If your children would rather do their work at night and leave the day free for play, let them! There is no one size fits all approach in homeschooling.

The trick of course is to figure out your personal template. Every spring day is not the same, nor is every night or day. Add your personal signature to the template after you've refined it. And simplify your homeschooling.

*

Let's talk about how to get started building a template. First of all, what is a template? In its most basic form, a template is a plan. But it's not an exact plan. It is just the *bones* of a plan, the shadowy outside lines. If you're a sketch artist, a template is what you would draw before you used darker lines. It is the shape or the outline of your main schedule.

My first brush with a template before homeschooling occurred the day my husband and I began a financial budget.

What a mess it seemed. So many bills! No uniform paychecks. To top it all, there were those pesky bills that came at different times of the year – some annually, some monthly, some bi-monthly and some at some random moments of the year that could only be remembered by mnemonics. (**N**o **D**arn **F**ooling **A**round – Due in **N**ovember, late in **D**ecember, due in **F**ebruary, late in **A**pril. Those are your property tax bill installments. You're welcome.)

The task seemed huge if not impossible.

I was supposed to turn this tome of numbers and data into a coherent whole that could be understood and, more importantly, controlled? What did I look like? Super accountant woman? Look! There in the spreadsheet! It's the gas bill! It's the mortgage! It's expenses! Down, down and balanced!

Later (much later!) when I finally got a handle on it, I realized that managing time was a lot like managing money. And the first step to knowing where it was going was to take a good long look at the regular expenditure.

As in budgeting money, there is little to be gained in trying to save time without knowing the amount that is currently being spent. With three children in tow, it takes us longer to get ready to go anywhere, so it helps to know how much longer and set aside a time budget for it.

This time budget must be worst case scenario, not best case. There will be so-called "last minute" spills and diaper changes. Someone will begin a fight with someone and discipline will be necessary. Budgeting for worst case scenario is the only way, in my experience, to never be late.

Often, we try to fit our daily routine into someone else's time arrangement only to feel like colossal failures. I would argue that this is like trying to download a financial budget of someone else's income and try to make it fit. It's just not going to work.

There are only 24 hours in everyone's day but there are individual routines, personalities and, for lack of a better word, family cultures we encounter. Some families take their food seriously, some don't, for example. Some take longer for school, some take naps, others play video games. The same 24 hours must be divided according to what we want to accomplish and how long it takes us given the personalities of the children and the adults with whom we live.

The first step then is not to save time or even to manage it. The first step is backwards: observing and noting how long it really takes.

Budgeting is a necessary step, but it's the *second* one. This is the beginning, then, of an individual template.

I had a friend in school who didn't understand how to take notes. She would listen to lectures and try to write down every word, which was impossible.

"Just write down what's important!" I told her. "It's simple!"

"But how do I know what's important?" she asked.

She hadn't taken the first step, which in this case was to research the kind of questions most likely to be on the test. Without that necessary research, it all seemed important and therefore overwhelming. Without taking an inventory of how long it takes us to accomplish a specific task, especially the repetitive ones that are so common in our lives, adopting any time table or schedule will be doomed to failure.

So, take a step back. Research.

It's the most effective way to begin. As you do this, you will begin to have the start of a personalized template. If you need more help in this stage of researching your specific style of teaching and your children's style of learning, I suggest you pick up my book *Create Your Own Homeschooling Curriculum*.

*

Now that you're taking a look at your day and how it already is and are working toward a general template, you should consider the important step of intention.

I've been reading *Game Changers* by Dave Asprey and one of the things he mentions in one of his first interviews (the book is a compilation of the best advice he received from people successful in their respective fields) is intention.

Setting your intention comes *before* planning. This is the idea behind setting aside time to dream. When your intention for the day or the week, month, or year is clear, organizing it becomes easier.

Without setting an intention of what you want to achieve, organization becomes ridiculously hard. It doesn't need to be set in stone, but a general idea is helpful.

Do that first. And only then, add or remove things based on your goals. Once your intent is clear, be ruthless about eliminating distractions and extraneous items.

Okay, now we are ready to make some progress. To recap, here's what we have so far:

1. Intention
2. Time budget
3. Template of homeschooling day

And yes, I do realize I mentioned these backwards when I just talked about them, but there was a reason for it.

And that reason was elimination. When you homeschool, a huge aspect is going to be getting rid of things. I cannot emphasize it enough. You have to learn to let go to stay sane.

Let's get into it.

*

Growing up, I never understood why my parents did not like me saying I couldn't find something. Now that I have children of my own, I get how annoying misplacing something can be.

Just yesterday, I ordered a garbage bag because the kids were going through the closet where we keep school supplies and were unable to find what they needed. Yes, a garbage bag – because the first thing you must do when you can't find something is start throwing things away.

So perhaps in math, you get to add before you subtract, all you PEMDAS fans. But when it comes to curriculum or teaching styles or even for simple sanity's sake, it makes sense to subtract before you add.

This is not just true when homeschooling in a small house. While it is necessary in a small house to keep clutter down, this is an effective tool no matter what size of home you have.

It makes sense to get into the habit or removing before adding in almost every situation that demands space – mental, physical or temporal.

When should you do this? How about at the time of year when you're looking at the new homeschool year? When many homeschooling parents are excitedly making lists, looking over other homeschooling parents' lists and searching online for what to add to their schedule, it's a good time to remember to remove something.

Look, I get it: I love research. And if some books and classes are good, more should be better, right, the thinking goes. But wait. Before you add anything to your schedule, consider removing something else.

Because we have limited storage in our home, our rule for bringing anything into it is pretty strict – there has to be a place we can put it before we buy it and we have to eliminate one other thing.

This is especially true of clothes and books. We choose to donate an equal amount of each. So if I buy a bag of books from a library sale, I have to donate a bag.

While this is good for frugal reasons, when it comes to planning for homeschooling, this idea works wonders. This year, when you decide you want to add something – an activity, a workbook, a read aloud, consider two things: where will it go in your day and in your home? Also, is there anything you can remove before you add it in?

Do that first. Before you add, subtract.

So now you have your template. You have a time budget that you set with your intention, you have a general idea of how you intend to run your homeschool day.

Try it out.

If it doesn't work, remove something. Then add something else. Change it up. Try new things. The best time to try different ways of doing things is when you're starting out.

Don't decide anything just yet. Play around with your template. What works? What doesn't? Just leave enough time to play with each, so as to give yourself and your children enough time. Also, do remember that the children will change and grow and your template will as well.

The only constant is change and nowhere is this truer than in homeschooling.

*

Having said that change is constant, I want you to consider that there is more than one way to organize a homeschooling day and more than one way to get an education. With that in mind, I want you to consider these two, short, opposing asides that follow.

*

What Unschoolers Can Learn from School at Home Types

Debate is unavoidable.

I was recently looking for a history curriculum for the children. We like our current approach, but I was considering a timeline or just a broad overview even if it was just for myself that would serve as a jumping off point so to speak. So, I started to read some reviews of the bestselling curricula and, you know what struck me?

There is no consensus.

None at all. There is only a trend. There is a majority and there are averages, but none, not one curriculum, textbook, author, style, gets a unanimous vote.

Some people didn't like the tone in Susan Wise Bauer's *History of the World*, some people did not like what they saw as the Christian bent in it, others went with E. H. Gombrich's book but it was rife with talk of millions of years, something that didn't sit well with others; still more people argued that much of what was in the history books was NOT how it happened at all.

Debate, disagreement, differences were, indeed are, unavoidable. They're unavoidable because there is no one-size-fits-all approach to teaching and definitely no straightjacket way of learning.

I recently attended a homeschool convention where I forced myself to listen to speakers I didn't agree with. In my experience, hearing the opposing point of view does one of two things – it makes you defend your point of view, at least to yourself, which requires that you address the questions head-on, and so gives you greater assurance that what you're doing is right, or it makes you see what needs to change in your own approach.

I decided to welcome the challenge. I believe other unschoolers would be wise to do so as well.

Here are five things unschoolers can learn from those who are more "school-at-home" minded. (Hear me out. Trust me, the other side of this argument follows this one.)

1. Punctuality

One of the biggest areas where the let's-do-school-at-home type of parent succeeds over an unschooling one, I believe, is in matters of punctuality. I remember getting an Uber ride from a mom who had homeschooled eight kids and she joked about how when her son entered the military, he said, "I love it, mom! It feels just like home!" She expected them to be ready, pencils sharpened, books out, to do school work at a specific time.

Another mom would send her kids out the front door and bring them in from the back door, wish her a good morning and then get down to teaching them – all this just to create a separation, to let the children know that this was serious, this was important and it was now time to learn – formally.

Unschoolers, typically, do not emphasize this kind of punctuality. Since learning takes place all day, they do not set aside time to learn, free from distractions within the normal day. I believe this can potentially become a flaw and the unschooling model can be bent to accommodate formal learning while leaving enough free time for the rest of the day to explore and continue learning by unschooling.

2. Systematic thinking

When I started looking for a history curriculum as I mentioned above, I did so for a specific reason. The children were being exposed to learning opportunities all the time because of the books they were reading, the television they were watching and the questions they asked. So, they were immersed pretty regularly in information and knew, excuse the redundancy – a lot about a lot.

What they lacked, and still do, were information hooks.

I find history fascinating because I have a general sense of what happened in each century and each period. They don't. As such, to them, everything happened a long time ago. And while I understand they are still young and much of this understanding will come later, I want them to have a system on which to hang all they will be learning.

This is aided by clear, definite, slow progression, not unlike learning math. It is only when enough of these appear that they can cross-reference and have fun gathering and sorting new information, i.e. learn.

3. Discipline

I've been reading how children do not need to be taught to read and elsewhere about how playing is more important than doing math. And while I agree with most of the points made in those articles, especially the ones that emphasize not pushing children too early because reading and writing is linked to big developmental changes in children, I see teaching or guiding as fundamental to learning.

Discipline in any area is basic. This is a fact of life that can be ignored only in fantasies and movies. While it is wonderful when we hit upon the one thing where we are gifted in a certain area and then find a way to build on it, the idea of the noble savage is far from truth. Children (and adults – not singling out kids) do not do hard things if hard things are not emphasized. That emphasis can come by habit or necessity.

Reading is hard, math is hard, learning a musical instrument takes work. Learning often takes determination, grit, sweat – all just different words for discipline. This is an area where school-at-home types strengthen their will and teach their children to do the same far more than unschoolers.

4. An emphasis on guidance

Teaching my children does not make me the source of all knowledge, but it does establish me in their minds as someone to look toward to guide their learning. In the information age, I see this as imperative.

The reason unschooling works well for many in the younger ages, is because, I think the parents' authority is already well established in the child's mind and he clearly depends on them for daily needs.

As a child grows up, these bonds loosen a little, and while that's a good thing, they still have a need for guidance. If parents do not provide this, something or someone else does. It happens all around you.

It happened to me – I went to private school; from the age of three, as soon as I left my home, all my affections, all my honor, toward my parents transferred over on to my teachers. My parents faded to the background – they didn't know much, I didn't see them all day, and they weren't dressed as well as my teachers.

The school at home people have this one correct. They establish themselves as the children's guides early and often. As such, the bonds loosen as they should, but don't break. They are not replaced by other authorities, of which currently there is no lack.

5. A rewards system

Unschoolers tend to look down on any kind of rewards system – they despise encouragement in the form of stickers, stars, or even cash, seeking joy as the only motivator for learning.

However, for better or worse, rewards and punishments are an inherent fact of life, just like work.

Rewards change, of course, as children grow and become adults – I have yet to see a 15-year-old get stickers for using the bathroom correctly or sit in the corner for jumping on couches after being expressly prohibited, but they do remain all through our lives. Unschooling parents need not shun them. They can instead teach the children to be guided by the right things. Rewards and punishments are just a way to hasten learning or natural consequences. Habits can start for one reason and continue for a completely different reason.

Yes, I know my unschooling friends are squirming at that. So here's the other side of the issue. I see no sense in being wedded merely to a philosophy – I would rather teach my children the best way they will learn. As such, take from these posts what you will and do what works for your family. There is no right answer.

*

What School At Home Types Can Learn from Unschoolers

I have written much about unschooling as a style that appeals to me in teaching my children. But I have a caveat – I also see the benefits of Charlotte Mason, Montessori and the Classical types of education. Here's the unique perspective unschoolers bring to the table.

1. Education does not always happen at age appropriate times.

The school mentality often makes people think that learning must happen at age appropriate times.

"What if my kids don't get it?"

"What if my kids are behind?"

"What if they can't understand?"

These are fears that plague new homeschoolers.

I would contend that they do so because they have been raised with the idea that at certain ages children learn certain things. With the push for earlier and earlier schooling, many parents worry if their children do not walk in lock step with their peers.

But wait. Education doesn't work like that. There is no set time for learning anything, and in fact, in many cases, later is far better than earlier.

Unschoolers instinctively get this. They're not interested in institutionalizing learning.

Unschoolers understand that teachers do not have some magic ability, that they — you! — can learn to gather all the strength, all the patience and resolve to teach your child at the pace he or she learns best.

As a result, they are challenged, but not frazzled by their homeschooling days. They know that even when it doesn't seem like school is in session, education and learning has never stopped.

2. Education does not happen in one place.

Have you heard of car-schooling? How about waiting room schooling? Coffee shop schooling? Park schooling? How about grocery store school? And I'm not talking about field trips when no one is paying attention, either.

In addition to these rather obvious scenarios, we can also add the fact that children truly are learning all the time.

If you are not actively teaching them something or feeding their minds with something all the time, they are learning something else, but they *are* learning.

They are learning while wiggling and not just from their textbook. Unschoolers understand this and try to create an environment where twaddle is kept to a minimum, so as to provide a rich environment – not just for the children but the entire family.

3. Discernment is an important skill even for children

This is perhaps the most important aspect of unschooling. Since children are learning all the time, discernment is a skill they need to pick up and pick up early.

I will admit this was not something I learned until much later because I was not taught how to separate truth from falsehood. I was given a textbook and tested on it and I was good at studying, so I thought I knew the truth.

I was wrong in the worst way possible.

Children *do* need facts – they do need to memorize and soak up facts, data, information, language patterns, poetry, history and so forth, but they also need a strong dependable gauge to measure these against. And they need to understand how to discern the truth.

This is an important distinction, I believe, and one that is the most useful aspects of homeschooling if the children are to be of practical use as adults.

4. You are unique and irreplaceable and so are they!

The biggest problem with the school at home approach is that it gives the impression that it seems easily copied. It doesn't matter who is doing the teaching, it doesn't matter who is learning, as long as the textbook is the same. This is patently false.

You as a parent are unique; your children are themselves; they are all different from each other. If you miss that, you are making the same mistake that schools make every day, which is the reason you chose to homeschool in the first place!

Unschoolers see this and will do nothing to squash the child's unique personality. While children still need discipline (and so do parents, if any education is to be accomplished!) we are not elves in Santa's workshop churning out toy cars. No one else can do what we do in the way we do it. Sure, they can learn something another way elsewhere but the reason they are with us is that we want to accomplish not just the end product but also control the method in which it is to be accomplished!

The manner in which education is imparted teaches children volumes about their innate worth, their choices and the adults they will become before you have even uttered a word.

So, now that you've read the two opposing views, what are you? An unschooler, a school-at-home type or something in between?

But wait! Don't rush to make up your mind. You don't have to be wedded to a philosophy just yet. In fact, the more fluid you can be when it comes to homeschooling, the better. It was this openness that made me come around to classical unschooling as our family's style.

If you'd like to know more about that style, please pick up my book *The Classical Unschooler* where I lay it all out subject by subject.

*

Okay, one more caveat before we leave the issue of templates and move on to quick time management strategies and that is the issue of being attracted to the difficult. I considered leaving this out of the book, but I think it's important and needs to be in here and it must be said.

Just because something is difficult, it does not follow that is good or even desirable as a goal. Just because a story, a book or a poem is hard to read, a game tough to play, a skill particularly hard to acquire, it does not then mean that it should be on a teaching curriculum.

There seems to be a bias in learning. The more difficult a challenge is, the more it finds its way into school planners.

In graduate school the hardest books are the ones with the most bragging rights. *Finnegan's Wake*, anyone? The harder it is, the more it entices us.

Why this preference for what is arduous, for what constantly calls on us to reach inside for Herculean strength? The things that make people successful on a daily basis are not onerous.

In fact, everyday life – at least modern life – is easy if incredibly tedious and unfortunately repetitive. Answering emails, fixing broken things, solving problems, paying bills, sweeping, doing dishes, even homeschooling. This is not especially hard.

Showing up is half the battle. Following through is the other half. Somewhere in the middle, the magic happens – work gets done. A life is lived, the day is won.

Knowing this then, why do we say to our kids that they should constantly be doing what is especially demanding? Why the preference for the most challenging curriculum? Why the bias against what they can enjoy as they learn? Why shun graphic novels?

Why not work to their strengths instead of constantly probe their weaknesses?

Why, oh why, does everything have to be a freaking challenge?

Do we live like that? I can tell you that the hardest thing I do lately is read all I can about running a website and weightlifting – two of my favorite subjects. I'm not jumping over hurdles to read books about math – a subject that I appreciate, but not one that interests me as something I would like to pursue.

Sure, the occasional challenges are good.

I make time to cook food because I know it's important, but dinner gets relegated into the realm of habit. I do it quickly enough to avoid it becoming a real trial. I try to make it as pleasant as possible, as easy to get done as I can. I listen to podcasts that I find interesting or music to keep me going.

Why then, when it comes to the children, do we place innumerable rules on them, most of which are designed to do nothing but challenge them at every turn? The marshmallow test anyone?

Whatever are we hoping to prove? That they can rise to every difficulty life will throw their way? That the world is cruel and they had better learn now how to constantly tell themselves no?

Willpower is like a muscle. It's not a bad idea to train it, but when every task – academic or otherwise – is chosen only for its difficulty factor, we can hardly blame children for giving up and hating to learn. This post explains quite well the options we have when it comes to training and educating children as well as ourselves.

Simple things motivate us, if only for their simplicity. Habits guide us, automating behavior. Occasional challenges are fun, even desirable, but we're not – by any means – raising Spartans.

Toughness is overrated.

TIME MANAGEMENT STRATEGIES

Now let's get into the nitty-gritty section of this book. This is the part where I share some quick, short, very practical ideas about how to fit things into your schedule. I tend to be one of those people that finds I have to achieve something on a fairly regular basis to feel good about myself. While vacations sound nice, it is always in the everyday doing of things that I find I am happiest. (I know, I sound like a hoot. Lots of fun at a party.)

Let's jump right into them.

First off, though, something to think about: what does a deadline, a block of time and a budget have in common? Answer: They're all limitations.

When you first begin homeschooling, or even consider homeschooling, you bump up against these limitations. And unless you begin to see them as goalposts rather than boundaries, it is easy to feel hedged in.

Consider this. Under certain circumstances, we love putting ourselves into situations where we have to attain something by a certain time, where at least for a while, we play by rules that require us to reach outside of ourselves. Consider games, competitions, challenges. Even ones we engage in for entertainment, like Scrabble.

So, for a while, we accept the rules, the boundaries and use them to propel us to become more creative and actually have fun in the process.

It's the same with homeschooling.

When faced with too many possibilities, it is easy to get overwhelmed. What do I want to learn? What do I want to make for dinner? What should we do today?

Answer: everything!

Limitations, like a financial or budget or a written schedule, give me a template and some options. Even if I ultimately reject them, these limitations give me a starting point. Limitations actually enhance our lives, even if they are for a short amount. Hitting a goal feels good. Living within a budget feels like a victory. Limitations can be friends.

This is exactly why we love classical unschooling. Unschooling feels too vast and classical learning way too excessive.

Here's the thing, though. You have to figure out that sweet spot for you. Too much lack, too much competition, too much scheduling begins to feel like a prison. So just because a little pressure works, be careful of adding more.

The best place to be is in right in the middle of that tension where the challenge is more or less matched to your (and your child's) ability. Find that sweet spot and stick with it.

Embrace your limitations and use them. Don't think of them as something to be overcome.

I spent far too long feeling sorry for myself when we started homeschooling. I considered how I wouldn't have time to myself, how the children always needed my help and hand holding and how I would never be able to gleefully make plans for the beginning of the school year in the fall like so many of my Facebook friends whose children are in public school did.

What I didn't realize is that those very same limitations gave me and my children the freedom to pursue things they would never have learned if they were away all day – practical, real world skills. And those same limitations gave me the life I wanted with my children. We learned to get along. We learned to stay out of each other's hair. We learned to use the time to develop our own talents instead of being directed by other people and institutions. We asked good questions and discovered unique answers. We talked. A lot. I wouldn't give any of those up for a day sipping margaritas by the pool.

So don't bemoan your boundaries. Learn to love them. They make you better.

*

Open any book on habits and sooner or later (sooner, in most cases) you will come across the admonition to "be consistent."

Then will follow reminders to wake up earlier and "eat that frog" earlier in the day. And perhaps a reminder or two to join an accountability group to stay on track.

There's only one problem with this advice: it may not work with your personality. But that's only a problem if you let it be one.

"Consistent" doesn't have to mean "daily."

When scheduling our homeschooling, I make sure to leave time for goofing off. I do this because I know I need it as much as the children do. And even with that we find ourselves dumping the schedule and running off to play on some days.

When I check out books from the library, I include some that look interesting, but once I take them home, I do not put restrictions on myself to read them all. And since we can check out 30 at a time (not including ebooks) I don't have to restrict myself. If they seem interesting, I take them home, but I am not committed to reading them all. I know I will quit some after the first fifty pages because they don't hold my interest.

At any given time, I have about five or six obsessions running through my head. My current ones are writing, frugality, reading history, brushing up on the two foreign languages I know, and lifting weights.

But I don't do all these daily. In fact, the moment I try to establish some sort of a schedule to be able to "be more consistent" with these interests, they become a little tiring.

But I suppose a caveat is necessary here. I'm not saying *everything* in your homeschool has to be the result of passion. And I'm certainly not mouthing platitudes such as "follow your bliss."

But I am making the point that it's okay to relax a little when it comes to scheduling your children in their endeavors. Consider longer timelines - weeks, months, years.

Not days. When planning, try to have a longer timeline in mind. As long as something gets done over a month, don't worry about the day to day work.

Most interests tend to be cyclical. Your desire for consistency does not need to take on the mantle of a dictatorship to be fruitful.

My daughter will eventually come back to cartooning and writing, even if she takes a break from it for a few days. I'm certainly not going to ask her to do it every day. Yes, she loves it, but if I force her to pursue that interest in a top-down way, she might just grow to hate it. I know I would.

While scheduling for passions and interests, be sure to leave room and time, not make appointments and programs.

Consistency doesn't always look consistent from the outside. And it certainly doesn't have to be daily to be effective.

But this is hard to believe and harder to explain. A friend of mine asked me yesterday, "How do you do it all? How do you read and homeschool and work from home? And work out and manage your blog? Do you sleep at all?"

I can't tell you what a well-timed, genuine compliment that was, because just that morning, under the influence of tiredness and PMS, (I should write a book on this! I am amazing three weeks a month and a complete potato for a week. Only, a cranky potato with thorns and an ice cream spoon.) I had been beating myself up for not ever having accomplished anything in my life. I breathed a little easier as I responded.

Here's how:

So I told her my "secret." Here it is. It's that I don't do it all every single day. Currently, I have two or three things that I call non-negotiables. These must get done every single day, or at least five days a week. These include homeschooling, writing, and working out.

Everything else is time batched.

Time batching is a productivity hack that groups similar activities together, so you can concentrate completely on them. It's the same idea behind cooking once a week or once a month and it's the same promise behind writing five or six blog posts at a time.

I take it a little bit farther, however. Because I tend to have a bit of an obsessive personality, I like to focus on my current obsession a little, well, obsessively. As a result, if I'm tackling reading, I will read a book a day until I'm sick of it and move on to binge watching a show. You get my drift.

The fact is some things require daily consistency, some don't. But because we hear "Do it every day!" or "Do it first thing in the morning!" or "Be consistent!" so often, we think we have to be an automaton moving from the first item on our checklist to the next.

We do not. We have more freedom than we think.

Find your non-negotiables and cycle through the rest. Get it done.

By the way, if you're looking to develop some great habits, get a copy of Charles Duhigg's book *The Power of Habit*. It's an excellent, interesting book and in it, he talks about a technique called sandwiching amongst other beneficial strategies for time management.

He explains how developing a new habit sometimes can be jarring. (Anyone who has started a new exercise routine, a new job, even a new year's resolution knows this.)

He gives the example of how radio stations usually introduce new songs into their repertoire. Sometimes, he says, the effect of a new song is so jarring, that even though it is to be liked by almost everyone, just because it was new, it is rejected. People switch radio stations.

Why is this? Simply because it is new. Just like a new habit, it feels uncomfortable. It is different.

So here's what you do: sandwich it into your schedule.

Find two things that are normal in your routine. Say, coffee and a shower. Then add in the one new thing you wish to do between them. Say journaling or reading or working out. Wake up just fifteen minutes early to leave time for that extra activity.

Do your first (habitual) activity, set the timer for fifteen minutes and do the new activity. When the timer goes off, stop and move on to the second (habitual) activity.

Voila! You just sandwiched something in. You did what radio stations have been doing for years by playing new songs in the middle of two well-loved songs.

Sandwiching as a technique has endless benefits for homeschooling and for other random tasks in your day. Especially ones you do not particularly like to do. I use it often.

*

Sometimes even the most well-meaning people can give us the worst advice. As I mentioned, doing something consistently does not mean that you need to do it every day. It's the same with pacing yourself.

Picture, for instance, beginning something new, realizing you're quite excited about it and then having someone else tell you, "No, just do a chapter today. Pace yourself."

Bad advice!

The problem with bad advice is that it always sounds so careful and so wise.

Well, yeah... I could get bored with this, you think. Perhaps I had better just read 50 pages a day. No sense in immersing myself in it today and getting bored tomorrow and abandoning it completely.

But have you noticed the disinclination self-directed learning has to pacing itself?

Self-directed learning - whether done by you or your children - follows its own rhythm. It is exciting, obsessive and not interested in external schedules. In fact, trying to get it to "pace itself" can hinder it more than help it.

Think about the last time you had a burning question - an online argument, for example. Or a conviction you couldn't shake. Or a book you couldn't put down. How much faster did you learn and how much did you retain from it?

I can almost guarantee you learned more in a day from your obsession than you would have had you done a little a day every day.

Here's what to do instead. Work as much as possible with your natural inclinations and let the children do so as well.

Craft a curriculum that works with their individual personalities. Let them be bored.

Realize that interest is cyclical and goes through waxing and waning cycles. If they're obsessed with something and then lose interest, it might come back soon.

Don't push for mastery too soon. To develop what we call grit, children need to try out a few different things and play at them before they're ready to settle in and work hard at it.

Instead of forcing a top down philosophy of learning and education, try to trust your own organic sense of self direction and see if you can work with it. Don't pace yourself. Go all out. Exhaust yourself. Then recover, refresh and come back.

That's how the best learning occurs.

A few months ago, I wrote a blog post about juggling well inspired by Michael Gelb's book *More Balls than Hands*. In the book, he differentiates between two management styles. He calls them the "project finisher" and the "time allocator," adding that the latter is far more efficient than the former.

Now I understand that when you're not "pacing yourself" you are more likely to be in a project finisher kind of role. But there are also days when the sense of incompleteness can be irritating and depressing. I am editing this book at the end of April, for example, and I just want to be done with everything – school, writing, everything. I want summer and I want a break. But it is not going to all get done in a day and expecting it to get done immediately can just lead me to frustration.

So I began to think of ways I – a natural project finisher could incorporate aspects of time allocation into our routine.

The easiest way to do this is by using a checklist.

If you're one of those homeschoolers who loves to finish a project, a checklist can be incredibly helpful. I have mentioned the importance of a template in our schedule before. Topping off that schedule with a checklist might just be the icing on the cake.

Why?

There are a few reasons this works. As someone who likes to see things get done and stay done, a checklist just feels right. There are people who are happy to touch a project here and another one there and let go. But I am not one of them. At least, leaving things undone leaves me with a sense of incompleteness. That translates itself into stress.

A checklist resolves that stress. Checking something off (or giving the children a sticker – or signing off on something – anything that works for your family) helps incredibly in managing my time. I know I will do the same tomorrow, but at least for today, the task is finished.

*

Speaking of scheduling and planning on a very practical level here, how long to homeschool is another big question that comes up quite consistently.

"Just two hours a day? Is that enough?" my father asked me once.

His seventy-five-year-old voice was still firm halfway across the world. I had just told him how our homeschooling was going and he was curious, a little doubtful but more skeptical than anything else.

Just two hours, I had replied, thinking, this will never make sense to him.

I went to private school, beginning at age 3 and I loved it. I excelled at it.

I'm not sure if I liked my school then because I was good or the other way around but school was like my second home. I certainly spent most of my day there. Beginning in first grade I left my house at 7:30 a.m. and didn't return until 4 in the afternoon.

Some of that was just commuting to school and back. Then there was recess and lunch break and time for down time even during classes, but I understood what my dad was asking – Is it enough?

Look, I get it. Frankly, I struggled with this question for years. But then I realized school was not something separate and discrete from life. Education was something you did in the midst of everything, not in the absence of living. What's the point of knowing how to read a textbook if you can't read a stop sign? Learning is practical, so what we do as sit-down schoolwork is the very basic reading, writing, math that lays the foundation of everything else. That basic foundation doesn't take longer than two hours a day.

But I completely understand the question because it is a question life throws at everyone – is it enough? Did I do enough? Did I earn enough? Did I get enough sleep? Enough protein? Did I read enough? Have I done enough work today that I can be content within myself to rest now?

Is it enough?

I remember when I quit my real estate work-at-home job to be a fulltime mom. My daughter had just turned two and my middle son was then eight months old. I remember asking myself if it was enough to say enough – that I was working as much as I could and was beginning to get overwhelmed. It was okay to step back and admit I was human, limited, finite.

But more time in school does not always equal better education. All I include into our homeschool attendance records is what I can document and test. But a good education encompasses so much more.

A good education does not necessarily break down into subjects, compartmentalized, organized, tested, completed.

Add to that the fact that I have no idea what skills the children will need in the future. Sure, there are the usual reading, writing and arithmetic – our heaviest emphasis at present. But beyond these two givens, I think of their education as something organic and eclectic. They are learning all the time, not just at special moments we are sitting together, pen in hand, eyes on the paper or screen.

*

Every family has a personality. This is not just the accumulative personality of every person in the family. There is a note, a tone, if you will, to families and the best thing you can do as a homeschooler is to work in accordance with that tone and not do anything drastically different from it.

If you wish to really get into the nitty gritties of personality types, Gretchen Rubin's writing has really helped me in this regard. I have figured out, for instance, why things that work for most do not work for me. In addition to identifying and working with your individual bent, she also goes into specific strategies that work to set up and maintain good habits.

One of the strategies she mentions in her book *Better Than Before* is the strategy of convenience. Rubin says that she takes the elevator in the gym. Now, at first, this seems counterproductive. After all, aren't you at the gym to exercise? And isn't taking the stairs part of the exercise?

But, she says, lugging her gym bag up the stairs is inconvenient. And if the elevator makes her going to the gym and being there more convenient, she is more likely not to dread it and actually get it done. It works.

This strategy has a direct application as I see it when it comes to scheduling and/or homeschooling.

When we first started homeschooling, I will admit that I was attracted to a more rigid schedule. I wanted my kids to know everything, do everything, be a part of All The Things. Over time, as I have seen them develop their own interests - slowly, but it has happened - these desires have diminished.

I no longer pick curricula for its difficulty. In fact, I work within the strategy of convenience and it works miraculously well for us.

Every time you change your schedule to suit your personality, you are using the strategy of convenience. We ease into the school week, choosing to read on Mondays rather than jump into complicated math.

Have you ever changed a curriculum halfway into your schedule to individualize it or skipped over a chapter here and there because it seemed easier that way? You are using the strategy of convenience.

So, here's what I recommend: find a way to ease into homeschooling. The more customized it is to your family, the more natural it will feel and the more likely you are to do it.

The easiest way I know to ease into homeschooling is by strewing. If you are just starting out, this is where you can begin and it won't even feel like you're doing anything.

I had a teacher in college who was opposed to entertaining her students in any way. She had a more serious disposition, if you will. Now, in all fairness, she was a great teacher and I don't want to complain about her too much. So let's just say that she had some very strong opinions.

This attitude has inadvertently found its way into my homeschooling. It is common for me to assume that if something is fun, that if the children are learning as well as enjoying themselves thoroughly, then they are probably not learning at all.

That nagging voice in the back of my mind shows up every time, watching, waiting it seems, for them to laugh and it goes, "Aha! See, this isn't school!" What a relief to know the voice is a liar, that children can indeed learn while playing!

In fact, research seems to suggest that it is in *play* that children learn best. And if you know me, you know that I don't think play is just for children.

I have learned so much without trying that I am realizing that just like the kids I learn best when I am focused, engaged and enjoying myself. Forcing myself to learn and study is necessary in certain situations but what gets me there is not external motivation but internal desire.

The enthusiasm to learn something new in which I am interested is an amazing and powerful force. This force can be harnessed especially in classical unschooling using the method of strewing.

So, what is strewing? The dictionary definition of strewing is to leave things about untidily. Ha! But the unschooling definition of strewing is to leave things out for children to discover and learn. Another way of looking at strewing is to suggest to children to notice things when you are out and about doing things together. Many parents do this unconsciously while out on the field trip or even around the house. This can be done by design.

As an unschooler, strewing comes in very handy when you are trying to either gauge the interest of the child or get the child interested either as an introduction to a new subject or to go deeper into a subject that he is already working. Strewing can easily be used as a strategy and classical education.

Now it might seem as if classical education with its focus on systems and specific ways of teaching can be completely opposed to the idea of strewing which seems haphazard and random. But it is not. Strewing can easily be incorporated into classical education and incorporated quite effectively and efficiently.

Here are some ways in which you can include strewing into your school day. You might already be doing some of these unconsciously.

Library books: I love our local library. We go there every week and the children check out whatever they're interested in. It is a great way not just to get your child's interest but to let him get deeper into whatever he might be interested in. Our current haul included some books on the natural world around us, some graphic novels and some picture books. This fits the age group and the interest level of my children.

However, this is where the classical aspect of my teaching comes in. While I do not limit their choices in books and I will let them read whatever they're interested in to a degree, I do consciously also order books from the library and put them on hold. These are books based on what they have been speaking about or playing or studying that I think they will like.

Use the local library to learn the interests of their children as well as to give them more than just what you want them to learn. Picture books are fantastic for this. Encyclopedia are also a good choice. My children can spend hours looking at pictures of animals. They have picked up information about climates in different areas and names of places and habitats I have not taught them. All through strewing. Who knows where these bits of information will land them?

Audio books: In addition to the books I mentioned above, we also listen to quite a few audiobooks. You can find them at the library or you can buy them on Amazon or you can have friends loan you some.

The best thing about these is that there is no dedicated time that you need to listen to them. We listen to them in our most natural surroundings – the car. (Okay, I'm kidding about the natural surroundings, but we do like to listen to them every time we are in the car.)

We have listened to audio books about historical stories of real men and women, inspiring events, people, business books, Greek myths, Egyptian myths, animal stories, Arabian Nights, The Odyssey, you name it, there's a book about it.

Audio books are great for introducing children to new language, or getting the templates of specific sentences into their minds which is one way they learn to think clearly and get their point across better. Audiobooks carry all the benefits of a read-aloud without actually having to make time to sit down and read to them (which we did for a while) but audiobooks continue to do this when we do not or cannot find the time ourselves.

Music: If you think songs aren't effective, think again. Some children tend to be more audio-centric in the sense that they learn better by hearing. These children by hearing the same things repeatedly.

As annoying as it is to me, my daughter seems to learn in this way. So in addition to audiobooks I make sure that we have enough good things to listen to. While I don't mind exposing them to different kinds of music (the radio in the car is not banned) I also find that I can use this time to teach her math facts set to music, or historical and geographical facts which also are part of our curriculum. Music is my favorite "Oh by the way" learning tool.

Subtitles: Closed captioning isn't used as effectively as it could be. Most parents don't even think about this when they turn on the television. Leaving it on can help children read as they stare at their favorite characters. I like to leave it on especially when we are watching a movie that is not animated and perhaps something that is above their age range. Today, for instance, we watched The Lord of the Rings which I'm quite certain had words they had not come across in their usual books. (And no, I'm not talking about Elvish.)

Here's another way to use subtitles: older children learning a new language can watch a movie in English and turn on the captions in the language they're working on. I'm sure it's all gibberish at first, but soon, patterns emerge and things get learned.

*

Another simple, practical strategy to get a lot done without having to think too much about it is by using the technique of time linking.

Time linking works because it uses associations.

Associations are powerful drivers of action and memory. Ever feel compelled to eat or cook just because you smell food? Who can't recall an exact memory from years ago because of finding oneself in a childhood home?

This happens because that place or time has developed strong connections in our mind with a specific thing. We can use that same strategy to stay on track in our homeschooling.

If you think about your day, chances are you are doing certain things at specific times. For me, I have to write in the mornings. I work best that way. I can't, for instance, pick up a book and read at five in the morning and I cannot write at seven in the evening. In my mind, each of those time blocks are linked with specific actions.

It's the same with homeschooling. The hours between 9 a.m. and 11 a.m. are the hours when we deal with difficulties the children might be facing and move on to more involved work in science or history.

We don't do anything else during those hours. If we want to watch something that is related to those subjects, I still prefer that we wait until after 11 a.m. to get it done. It doesn't "feel" right to turn on the television before noon. In my mind (and in my children's minds) that time block is linked strongly with sit-down work.

It is best if time linking comes together organically, but that doesn't mean you can't impose any structure. Take your normal day and see how it unfolds naturally. Then see if you can tweak it a bit.

I will warn you against getting started too soon on this. Toddlers seem to march to the beat of their own drummer, so if you try to impose time linking on a toddler or preschooler, it could be rough. We don't do formal sit-down work until the child is ready, which is much later. Time linking for a toddler works for nap times and lunch/snack times. No more.

Customizing time linking to your schedule will get things done, but keep you from feeling like you have to be the one pushing your children to get things done. Instead, it will begin to feel habitual and incorporated into your lifestyle.

Speaking of time linking, I must mention here that I leave large swathes of time empty in the afternoons. And sometimes there are days when I do not schedule anything. Empty spaces are not just there because we couldn't find something to put there. Sometimes, I decline events to leave days blank. They are important to me.

Let me explain.

Most homeschoolers can gauge the general mood of the day by how the mornings go. At least after a while, we get better at predicting the micro-climate of the family, so to speak, for any given day. Just this morning, I had to break up a fight between my two sons. That's when I knew it was going to be one of those Mondays.

Sigh.

If you've been reading my blog *The Classical Unschooler* for a while, you know I write a lot about scheduling. I use time blocking and other techniques like momentum to get things done.

But all that aside, the one thing I am learning to account for is what I call the emotional load. You could also consider it the mental load. Even with all the time management ideas in the world, I have to leave room for this final piece or it all falls apart for us.

The emotional load, by the way, is something that never bothers my husband. Let me rephrase that. The emotional load *of the homeschool* is something that never bothers my husband. He has work stress, but he seems quite able to retreat into his mental cave as a reprieve from the children.

Call it the difference between the sexes or a difference in our personalities if you will, but I will fall apart sooner than he will when it comes to our homeschool.

So what's a homeschooling mom to do?

For one, be aware of your personality. If you're tuned into the needs of your children, sometimes it can be exhausting. Yes, I know some moms who can take it into stride, but I am not one of them. When I get overwhelmed, it is important for me to admit it and not gloss over it or ignore it hoping it will go away on its own.

Secondly, I have to take time for self-care, even if that means taking time off from homeschooling. Think about it. Every profession gets vacation time. If you are treating homeschooling as serious work, you need to take some days off. Scheduling them in is a good idea.

And lastly, ask for help. You cannot be Super Mom all day, every day. I mean, yeah, you're seriously amazing with all that you do, but it's okay to take a break once in a while.

When scheduling, remember to account for the emotional load. It's a big mistake to ignore it.

*

One of the "rules" of our classical unschooling method is that we expect passion. We assume that each of our three children will be passionately interested in something that is meaningful.

But here's the caveat: it has to be personally meaningful. It has to mean something for them.

As a result, we don't enroll our children in sports or music lessons unless we see interest.

So how do we teach interest? As it turns out, it's impossible to teach interest. You can only share it and see if they will take to it.

My husband is an amateur guitar player. He plays only what he likes and is completely self-taught. From the looks of it, he truly enjoys practicing. He finds a song that is about his level, learns how to play it online and stays with it until he has mastered it. He claims he has no talent. (I would disagree.)

My daughter expressed some desire to learn guitar, so we enrolled her in a class. But she had no interest in it, so we did not push it.

She does however watch me write this blog. And we read a lot together. So what does she develop an interest in but writing fantasy stories! An intuitive speller and strong reader, she has taken up writing stories as her interest.

But it takes time.

Unfortunately, this is one of those things that can't be pushed or rushed. My almost ten-year-old son, for instance, has almost no interests that we can discern yet. Okay, he loves playing video games and seems technically inclined. He has strong math skills.

We might introduce him to coding the same way we introduced my daughter to guitar. After all, we do want to help our children find their interests and it helps to introduce them to a wide range of them. I don't think any parent would disagree with that.

Where we part ways with most is in pushing them to learn something they have no desire to learn at all.

I have found that the best way to get our children interested is to have something in my own life I'm passionately interested in and introduce them to a variety of such things. See what sticks.

It really is as simple (and as difficult) as that.

*

January can be a rough month. It's cold and rainy or snowy; children are typically inside. The Christmas festivities have come and gone and there are resolutions to make. Family has usually come and gone and there's cleaning to do.

In the middle of this, picking ourselves up by our snow-soggy bootstraps is just not fun. Who wants to homeschool when the end of the school year is so far away and the beginning was so long ago?

But this is exactly why we begin our year in January.

Along with the rest of the world, we make our resolutions. We just have the smell of new books to go along with them.

You see, continuing something is incredibly difficult this time of year, but starting something new is just plain fun. We're motivated in January!

There's something about the prospect of no-holidays-no-disruptions in the air this time of year. I love it. It helps us settle into a good, strong routine.

As I've already mentioned, the weather creates an insular environment. We are looking for things to do at home. But this doesn't mean we can't play. Creating a new curriculum, picking new books to read, learning new things can include the element of play – inside – that often seems to be missing when back-to-school routines are mentioned in September.

Another good reason to begin in January? We have children with fall birthdays! I have children with birthdays in the latter half of the year: August, September and December. It makes little sense to us to follow the established school year.

For the most part, I stay apace of their development and their interests anyway, but even with my eclectic style, I like to know which grade they are most likely to fall into – if only to know when to stop pushing. The problem with eclectic schooling is that it is easy to push the children with extra work just because they can do it.

It makes far more sense to me to begin in January and sometimes (often!) be done by Thanksgiving.

Sometimes, I think that homeschoolers forget how much freedom we actually have. With the lack of boundaries and laws and rules, we tend to cling to what we have learned or what we see around us.

A question I often get when I mention we begin in January is how we keep records.

My answer is always, "The same way."

I simply write what we intend to do in the year – any year – and file the necessary paperwork. Even though we file when the state requires us to do so (October, in our case) it makes no difference to our curriculum or our homeschool.

*

Before I became a mom, I sold real estate for a short while and the biggest thing I learned in real estate was that the oft-repeated adage of location, location, location is true. You are better off buying a decrepit house in a great neighborhood than you are buying a beautiful model home in a not so nice area. That the rule about location, location, location is a perfect one when it comes not just real estate but also time management and also space management which ultimately leads to better time management. Let me explain.

First, space.

If you haven't had a toddler in your home for a while, you will notice that every glass jar, indeed every object in your home is sitting at exactly the wrong spot the moment said toddler walks in the door. I know this because years ago my parents rearranged our entire home when my nephew visited. I did the same as soon as my husband and I had children. Everything became too fragile or too dangerous. So it moved and occupied the higher realms of real estate a.k.a. shelves. As the children grew older however I began to then realize that certain things could then be moved lower to save me time.

I learned from one of my friends that their snacks could be placed in a strategic location at their height so that they could get to them and I didn't have to do the dispensing each time. Dishes could be placed on a lower location, so that the children could set the table. Cereal could be within the arm's reach of the oldest child so she could feed the rest breakfast. Simple changes in the kitchen helped save me time and get the children involved in basic tasks.

Second, the more direct aspect of location: time. I have found that placing a specific task in a different location of my day causes it to be done more efficiently, thereby saving me time in the overall day. Exercise, for instance, works best when it's sandwiched between a nap and cooking dinner. I know, it doesn't sound efficient, but that is where its perfect location lies.

Also, I recently learned from another friend that prepping dinner right after eating lunch and before washing the dishes from said lunch, saves an immense amount of time in preparing dinner. My energy levels tend to be lower in the evening and usually I want to relax with the rest of the family, so what gets done efficiently and quickly during the twelve o' clock hour can take at least another half hour in the five o' clock hour. Location strikes again.

If you're struggling with a specific task in your day, try and change the time or space location and see if there's a perfect fit. Chances are there is something you are not seeing just yet. Location, location, location works for more than just real estate.

SUBJECTS

In Defense of Busy Work

We're a pugnacious bunch, we unschoolers. And yes, that includes even classical unschoolers. We don't like worksheets and we hate wasting time.

Having given up on the idea of school at home, we reject everything that remotely smacks of a classroom with an almost iconoclastic glee.

Now, now, I'm not singling you out. Don't get defensive.

I speak here mainly of myself.

Lately though, I have simply begun to appreciate all over again the very specific benefits of time spent working on a problem. And that doesn't often happen outside of worksheets. Or memorization.

Now as my older children have entered that very difficult and rather hard to identify second phase of classical learning - the logic phase - I have learned to enjoy watching them think things through. I have also started to see how tedious this process can be.

There is, of course, no better way to showcase or learn thinking things through than in straightforward math. So we've been spending a lot of our homeschooling time lately at the computer solving math problems.

Sounds like busy work, my mind reacts.

So be it, I retort, and get back into it.

The second phase of our homeschooling might look a lot like a classroom on a bad day, and while I am certainly not trying to do school at home, learning to think things through is a worthy skill I do intend to push my children into one way or another.

Some days, we have tears. But most days, we also have a sense of accomplishment, a putting together of things hitherto unknown. Because if the goal of education isn't learning to put diverse things together to make sense of things hitherto seen as discrete, I don't know what is.

I am beginning to learn that some stuff we throw out as merely busy work can sometimes provide the mental space for higher order thinking.

How We Teach Math in the Elementary Ages

There's been a lot of talk about math anxiety lately. Apparently, parents have it and the fear is that we pass it on to our children. So say the Common Core pushers, anyway.

I found the opposite in a small but significant survey of my readers.

Here's how I started, however. I was one of those homeschooling moms who started too early. I remember poring over early curricula and then getting one for my daughter who was two at the time.

Yes, two. Go ahead, add me to the Homeschooling Hall of Shame.

I will readily admit now that it was a mistake. It was also incredibly frustrating. Even today, I find those counting bears in the couch cushions. And, no, they didn't help at all.

When I finally gave up and decided to wait a while, I thought I would go with a curriculum. It was fine at first and my daughter liked worksheets so it worked for a while.

The problem came when the curriculum required things to be done a certain way and that way only. And transitions from one kind of calculation to another, from addition to subtraction, for instance, had its own logic. Also, there was an attempt at moving toward algebra - algebra! - early.

Even if I understood the logic behind it, the children found math confusing and confusion was the last thing I wanted my children to get from the learning of math.

Even then, I tried to make it work. I rearranged the curriculum worksheets so they were more intuitive.

Eventually, however, I gave up trying.

I tried some alternatives. We used Khan Academy for a while, but I was bothered by the lack of rigor in their early years and the push to read graphs. The children did fine with those but stumbled over basic math facts.

So we entered a time when we would do math without a curriculum. I thought I would be scared. Instead, I felt an immense sense of freedom.

Finally, I was able to transition the children from addition to subtraction to multiplication to division in a way that was more intuitive to them. When I needed worksheets, I printed them out online for free. There were even a few websites I could have them practice math facts online.

I made my own flashcards. I put real world problems to them in a meaningful way. And it worked! It still works!

There is a logic - a flow if you will - to math. It builds on itself from simple to complex. You already know this. If your curriculum doesn't seem to follow it, you're better off without it.

Most Science Curricula is Quite Useless

Next to math, science is one of those things parents worry about teaching the most. I will admit to some trepidation myself. It seems like such a vast, broad field after all.

But here's the thing to remember: as with history, most science curricula you purchase (if you purchase one at all – we have in the past) is quite useless. When you know this and accept it, teaching science becomes much, much easier.

Let me explain.

Science is about inquiry.

The basic tenet of science, if you will, is the same as a Google search: "Let's find out." We frame the question, get information, see if it fits, reframe the question with new and old available information and reach a potential answer.

Unfortunately, with science curricula, we sometimes get the idea that there is a specific body of facts we have to know and if we don't know that (or don't agree with it), we don't know science. The corollary is that if we know that specific body of facts and accept them as complete truth, we are somehow now wedded to science and everything we say about it is, in fact, absolute truth.

Neither one of these perspectives is true.

While we have loved our curriculum in the past, we don't mistake it for fact. As someone who has spent hours researching the data on food in general and carbohydrates in particular, the idea of "settled science" does not appeal to me.

And while it is important to know some facts just as with history, it is even more important in science to be able to put them in perspective and think through them logically.

Also, consider that SATs and ACTs do not actually ask for science "facts" but only that the student can think like a scientist.

So you see there's nothing to fear. As long as you're willing to make mistakes and let your children be willing to make mistakes, experiment and find out, as long as you're willing to research and abandon ideas that don't logically follow, knowing that there is a long line of people who have done exactly the same thing before you, you're good to go.

How To Teach Reading and When

There is a new game that's being played at my house – the rhyming game. The children, it seems, are currently obsessed with finding words that rhyme with each other.

And it's not connected with reading exercises or anything. The kids do it as fun.

I don't know when this trend started but it's recent. I have to laugh at that because I distinctly remember rhyming as something that was always a struggle for both my older children. And here they are now. Not only explaining it to my (as yet) illiterate four-year-old but making a raucous game of it all!

When my oldest daughter was five, we started slow. We used *Teach Your Child to Read in 100 Easy Lessons*. As I said, we started very slowly. If we had problems blending sounds, we put the book away for a week or two and then came back. I did not push.

It was the same with my son. We did not do the writing part of the exercises. If you've seen *Teach Your Child to Read in 100 Easy Lessons*, you know what I'm talking about. (Highly recommended, by the way. It's simple, straightforward and short. But feel free to customize it.)

But the rhyming! Oh, the rhyming!

It was a struggle, to put it mildly. And they didn't get it. So we decided to skip that as well. I checked a few lessons down the road and was happy to discover the book dropped the rhyming exercises, so I didn't worry about it.

Teaching reading need not be scary!

Reading is one of the first things most homeschooling parents teach and I think this is where we either develop our deep confidence or think maybe we're not cut out to homeschool after all. In other words, teaching reading can make or break your homeschool.

Reading is also something children can and have picked up themselves.

So which is it? Is reading difficult or not?

Yes and no. If you start before the child is ready, it will be torture. A very wise homeschooling mom once told me to wait until they were ready. I am so glad I decided to take her advice.

She also told me not to rush after letter recognition, to start teaching reading only after the child was able to blend letters.

The best advice I received was to wait until my child was ready. But what's readiness? This is. Do this exercise. After and only after the child is proficient at sounding out letters, offer a two-letter word like "at" and see if the child can sound out the "a" and the "t" and blend them. If and only if he is able to do that, introduce a letter before the "at" to make words like cat, rat, etc.

If the child successfully blends these, congratulations, your child is reading and you can now proceed – gently – with other lessons.

The hard part, of course, is waiting. There is a push for children to learn to read earlier and it's easy to get caught up in that. But try to ignore that. While waiting, reading to them will be the most important thing.

If you have the need to introduce something reading-wise, I highly recommend *The Letter Factory* by Leapfrog. My kids watched this all the time and learned letter sounds very easily with it.

Teaching Writing

Next to teaching children to read, perhaps the next task fraught with stress and uncertainty is teaching writing. There are entire courses dedicated to how to write – ones that some homeschoolers swear by. And while my intention is not to deride any of those courses, I want to say that writing isn't hard.

Forget academic writing!

I have an MFA (a Master of Fine Arts) in creative writing. And I doubt I would have it today if I had pursued writing of the academic sort. From a very young age, I was interested in stories. I remember crafting poems and short stories since I was about eight or nine years old.

While I had some training in grammar, it certainly did not involve more than just the basics. I don't remember ever studying tenses. And I never diagrammed a single sentence. I had not been asked to cite another writer's work. I had no exposure to what we call "academic writing."

What I did get however is excellent exposure to good literature. And I loved to read. I read and experimented with different forms and voices in my writing. Suspense, mystery and crime novels gave me my plot and pacing constructions. I devoured these books, loaned to me happily by my older brother.

All this to say, if you're teaching your children writing, don't start with the academic. Start here.

<u>Three Strategies for Teaching Writing</u>

Strategy #1: Reading / Memorization / Copy Work

We learn in most cases by imitating. So it makes sense to read to children. Reading and memorization is the most basic form of putting templates of good writing into their heads so that construction of sentences and sentence structure become second hand to them.

To this, you can add copy work. If you are concerned about spelling or grammar, have them copy a few well chosen, well-constructed sentences from their favorite book of stories or poetry.

Strategy #2: Blogging

If they want to make the foray into slightly more serious writing, create a free blog and let them at it. If you do not wish for others to see it, keep it on a private setting. This is a great way to encourage them to put down their thoughts on paper, um… screen. It's also excellent typing practice.

My daughter has a blog that she updates off and on. It gives her a creative outlet and I will usually go over it with her and correct her errors when she's not feeling defensive. This is a great way to teach writing and spelling because it is she who is doing the asking and the learning and not me making her do it.

Strategy #3: Writing Stories / Copy Work

Another method to employ is one used by a friend of mine. For her more reluctant writer, she would type out stories he told her, as he told them. Then she would print those out and give them to him to copy by hand. When he saw that he actually had things to say that sounded interesting, he was more interested in writing.

Teaching writing doesn't need to be scary. Just be creative about it.

The Case for Starting With Bad History

Anyone who reads my blog knows I'm a lover of history. I often have book suggestions and lists for you to browse that I label "good" history. But today I want to deal with the relatively controversial topic of "bad" history.

You might ask *what* bad history? What's bad history, anyway? Usually, bad history is an event told from a place of bias. But I've been mulling over this idea in my mind that it is usually a good idea to begin learning where and when you can. Sometimes that begins with bias because you can't escape a certain bias in every writer – ancient or modern. Begin where you are is my motto. Of course you can't and don't – and won't – stay where you are if you read and study and learn enough.

Consider the boom in current historical fiction. Books and movies and Netflix shows – there is supposed history all around us. "But that's not how it happened!" and "Revisionist!" is the cry we often hear. And let's not forget "Fake news!" Surely, we should avoid bad history, right? I mean, it's a lie.

But wait, I say. Bias is inevitable.

We've been listening to the Histories of Herodotus in the car on drives while running errands. And while there is much that is informative in it, the true value of listening to

Herodotus is in the entertainment of it. History is a narrative, after all, and Herodotus manages to maintain a veneer of factual reporting while letting slip some pretty liberal use of "so I've been tolds."

All this to say bias is inevitable. No matter where you start, depending on where you stand, history looks different. There's no sense in denying it or trying to make it "fair."

In fact, it is in the trying that we most belie our biases.

So why not start there? Start with bad history, if you must. At least it gives you something to think about – something to sink your mental teeth into. Then go from there. Argue, sound out, find out. Learn and grow. Look at things from various perspectives.

Then create your own perspective. If nothing else, you will have worked your way through some fallacies and created an argument.

And in the process, you will have learned more than a simple rendition of the facts.

The Uses of Memorization

I just finished listening to a podcast by Tim Ferriss about memorization with Ed Cooke, Grandmaster of Memory. You can find the link on my blog *The Classical Unschooler* if you're interested in listening to it.

My children in elementary years have enjoyed memorizing and I have found that I often have had to provide no incentive for them to do so. They just liked it in itself.

Memorization, I have noticed, might be the one thing that divides the classical homeschoolers from the unschoolers more. If you speak to a classical homeschooling mom, chances are her children are memorizing everything from Latin words that make no sense to them to American Presidents. They are also quite well versed in uses of mnemonics and can recite a breathtaking array of poetry complete with actions and articulations that make you think you are watching a performance.

Unschoolers, on the other hand, typically shun memorization. This was incidentally the breaking point for me when I mentioned to a friend and fellow homeschooler that I was having the children memorize poetry. She claimed that no self-respecting unschooler would do such a thing.

So while listening to the above podcast, I began to wonder if there was any use to memorizing at all or was I interested in watching people like Ed Cooke simply because he was an oddity in the way people read about the amazing feats of, say Guiness World Record holders?

Was there any intrinsic benefit to memorizing information, I wondered, beyond just being able to regurgitate it on to your tests?

It is an important question. Anyone, given time and practice can get better at memorizing with some techniques. But the question is, as effective as these techniques are, what is the point? What are we going to do with all this information?

More importantly, in an age where information is available to us with simple voice commands, where encyclopedia are soon going to be as ubiquitous as putting on a pair of Google glasses, should we even be memorizing?

Doesn't the opportunity cost almost beg us to use our time elsewhere? Memorizing takes a fair amount of time and effort; aren't we better off using that time elsewhere?

Thankfully for me, the question was asked. And answered. And I am happy to say that I believe memorization still has a place in a person's life.

As a classical unschooler, I am more interested in giving my children the tools of learning (and making sure they use them often) than in covering any given curriculum. And I'm beginning to think that memorization is one of those most important tools. Yes, even with Google and Siri and what's-her-name.

Memorizing something, even a deck of cards, or a random list of numbers, according to Cooke, forces one to learn different ways of looking at things.

It forces you to categorize things differently in your brain. For instance, it makes you think of cards as people or of numbers as letters. This drawing together of disparate objects and putting them together in a different category than you would usually has a very practical application, even a personal one.

I think it is one I use almost instinctually and one that I usually get into trouble for. Maybe you do it, too.

Have you ever been doing something highly technical and then turned then inanimate thing you are working with into an anthropomorphous being in your head, maybe even someone you know? What did you do the next minute? You probably removed it from your mind! But that is exactly the kind of learning (because that really was a form of learning) you need to memorize and to have a rich inner life.

For that, dear reader, is where all this memorization work is taking you and your children.

Memorization isn't just about growing your brain, although it does that, it isn't about keeping your brain active into its older years, although it does that as well, memorization really is about making life more enjoyable, about making you more fun to yourself, a better person, a bigger person in your own being.

Isn't that what we all want anyway?

Because memorization forces you to learn to categorize, organize and remember information by changing its form, those skills can then be applied to things that are personal. How would you like to remember – in vivid detail a Christmas dinner you had with your daughter from years ago? And wouldn't you like to have the perfect memory of your first date with your husband? Taking the kids to Disneyland? Memorization can do that for you.

This isn't about history timelines or dead presidents. This is about learning skills and tools that can then be used to give yourself and your children a richer life, no matter what they do. It's something worth working toward.

CHALLENGES & QUESTIONS

We live in a small house. Is it necessary to have a dedicated schoolroom? How can I still make homeschooling work?

Before we started homeschooling, I made the mistake of wandering innocently onto some Pinterest boards for ideas. I say "mistake" because what I saw was immediately overwhelming. I saw dedicated school rooms! Imagine that … and keep imagining it, because for our little 1000 square foot house, it was just not going to happen. How in the world was I going to homeschool in our small house?

We have three bedrooms – the boys' room, the girl's room and our bedroom. Beyond that, there's a bathroom (a small one) and a dining area and living room.

Where in the world was my dedicated school room going to be with the pretty lettering on the walls? And the maps? And the kids' art work?

I was saddened. Perhaps you are, too. So here, I'm going to talk about what you do not need and what you do need when it comes to being able to homeschool in a small house.

First things first. You do not need a chalkboard. Yes, I said it, and you can quote me on it. The oddest thing about making the decision to homeschool is that most people think they need a chalkboard. (I can't tell you how bothered I was before I started homeschooling that I didn't have a chalk board on the wall.) So let me reiterate. You do *not* need a chalkboard. Or a dry erase board. I think the idea of school that looks like a classroom is something so deeply ingrained in our minds that we can't conceive of another way. But you're a homeschooler. So use paper. Heck, use whatever you have.

The advantage of homeschooling after all, is that you will be working one on one with your children. Use a pad of paper to explain a problem. Alternatively, if you really like dry erase boards, you can get a small one to hold.

I still much prefer paper.

Oh, here's another one: You do not need a dedicated school room. Yeah, I was sad that I didn't get to decorate one with maps and my children's art work, but in general that was the only part I missed. I soon realized I didn't need one.

If you have an extra room that you can turn into a school room, great, but you don't *need* one. There is absolutely no *need* for a school room or a play room for your children.

Yes, it's nice to be able to put all the "school work" in one room and yes, it's fantastic to be able to get all the toys put away out of sight in the evenings, but no, you don't need a separate room for that.

"School" tends to spill out into real life anyway, especially if you're an eclectic classical unschooler. So why bother trying to contain it in one room?

Writing? Use the dining table. Reading? Use the couch. Memorizing? Use the backyard or patio. Or the car.

However, when you get right down to the brass tacks, here are the things that you *do* need.

You will need a dining table that is clear of things. Many people have a dining table with things on it. At least a table cloth. It's a good idea to take some time to clear clutter before you begin homeschooling because it tends to collect. Keeping a small house clear of clutter is the single best thing you can do for your homeschooling success.

Alternatively, a desk and a chair in the kids' rooms where they can sit and write, read or do Lego projects could work as well.

Another good idea is to have a dedicated space or closet to store school supplies and books. We have a closet that my husband has built shelves in. In a small house, shelves are a life saver.

In this specific closet however, we keep only school-related things. Nothing else. It is accessible to the children and it is cleared out regularly. Anything that we are done using gets sold or given away or even thrown away. We do not store more than necessary.

A closet also serves us better than say, shelves, because at the end of the day I can put things away and *shut the door*. Because I am here all day long, in the middle of the toys and books, it's nice to be able to close it when I stop working.

Okay, the most important thing of all. You will need a couch. Most of our sit-down work happens at the dining table, but we do the occasional read aloud on the couch. (I've been reading aloud after lunch, so we like to just hang out at the table and listen.)

Most of the children's reading is also done on the couch and in their own beds. All this to say that if you are in love with reading nooks and can afford to have them in your home, that's great. But if you cannot, you're not robbing your kids of a lifetime of reading. If my children can read hanging upside down from two chairs, they can read in a brightly lit open living room.

Don't stress it.

And definitely don't let the size of your home stop you from taking on the adventure of a lifetime and giving your family the gift of homeschooling.

I cannot dedicate the same time to all my children! One of them takes up all my time. How do I homeschool?

My biggest frustration when it comes to homeschooling is not the questions other people ask of me. It's not about socializing the children or even what curriculum we buy. And no, it has nothing to do with whether we memorize or not.

My biggest hurdle with homeschooling is that my attention is not equally focused on all my children.

My daughter takes up most of my time.

A typical math lesson will go like this. I will show them how to work on something and give them some practice problems on our online program. My son will take what I have shown and run with it. He will make mistakes, but learn by doing. My daughter, on the other hand, will need me to sit next to her and teach her step by step until she does not make any more mistakes.

It's just a difference in their personalities.

Don't fight it.

The hardest thing for me to do has been not to fight this seeming inequality. I am just coming around to accepting that not everything has to be equal. They don't have the same personalities or learning styles. Why in the world would I assume that they would take the same amount of time or that my role would somehow be the same for both?

When it comes to the youngest, I intuitively and intellectually know that I will do things differently and that certain things will take more (or less) time. But for the two older children, the similarity in their age makes it harder for me to let go of my false idea of equality.

Not all children take the same time. Not all children need the same time.

It's okay to homeschool lopsided. Do what it takes. Sometimes, lopsidedness is what it takes to get the job done. So be it.

Are you making these curriculum blunders?

If you're like most moms who homeschool or are considering it, you are – to put it lightly – on it.

Before pulling out the sleeping bags and cleaning them for summer, you have scoured the catalogs, overwhelmed yourself with yet another Google search on homeschooling curricula, your Pinterest boards are full of ideas for the next three grades of schooling each child and you're even braving the Facebook homeschool curriculum groups, with PayPal on overdrive.

But wait.

Are you making one of these five biggest blunders?

Asking this question early can save you heartache, yes, but it can also protect you from spending thousands of dollars on curricula that will leave you unhappy, your kids grouchy and you hating the very idea of homeschooling.

BLUNDER #1 – Not taking the time to recognize your child's individual personality

Every child is different. As a mom, you already know this. You know which one out of your children is the social butterfly who chats with all the grocery store clerks and you know who is the recluse. You know your singers from your drummers and your – ahem – controlling ones from the kids who are happy to just follow along.

When you buy a curriculum, remember these differences.

For some reason, even though as moms we understand our children's unique personalities, as homeschoolers, we fail to acknowledge them. There is no one style that fits all and if we try to teach all our kids the same way, it's only a matter of time before we teach them to dislike learning.

BLUNDER #2 – Not understanding your own unique teaching ability

To understand your unique teaching ability, you have to first go back and think about what drew you to homeschool or unschool your child in the first place. What is your gift? What about having your child with you all day long resonated with you? What did you hope to achieve by this togetherness?

Think it through and try to formulate or find a curriculum that works in accordance with your vision.

There were months that I spent feeling guilty for not reading enough to my children, not doing what all my other homeschooling mom friends were doing. It was only after I took this quiz that I realized why I had been feeling like I was teaching differently from the others. Most of my friends followed the classical system; I was more of an unschooler.

Whatever your style may be, to avoid feeling like you've been put into a straightjacket, play to your strengths in what you choose to do this year.

BLUNDER #3 – Overscheduling your school days

This usually happens because either you're trying to replicate school at home or because you're just having tons of field trips and fun, fun, fun. If you (and your children) enjoy either of these, there's nothing wrong with it. But most of the time, children, especially younger than ten years of age (or the third-grade level) do not need hours and hours of sitting down and working at a desk. Some studies suggest that it could even be detrimental.

Leave room in your homeschool days for segues, for spontaneity. Leave room for fun.

Do not, I repeat for emphasis, do NOT schedule 180 days of school. Yes, I know, that's what the State of California requires, but trust me, if you teach them diligently, you will have 180 days of school even without scheduling them all. I would start by scheduling three solid months at a time.

After those initial three months, you can take a week off, review, and see what pace works for your family and plan the next three months accordingly.

BLUNDER #4 – Buying a premade curriculum for a specific grade level

Okay, okay, before you throw this book to the curb, unfriend and denounce me publicly, let me say this. Some homeschoolers do just fine with pre-packaged curricula. They find just the right one that works with their style of teaching, their children's style of learning and they don't hold so tightly to it that they can't veer off the beaten path ever so often.

However, the problem with a pre-packaged curriculum is that most moms are tempted to follow the guidebook that comes with it. If you don't follow the guide, you worry that you won't finish in time, aren't doing it right, and so on.

The other problem with pre-made curricula is that it often does not address children working a grade or two above or below their grade levels, which can happen often before middle school. My son, for example, started second grade math while he was at kindergarten grade level. Because I homeschool multiple children, I could accommodate his needs but if I was limited by our curriculum choice, I suspect he would be bore

Pre-made curricula takes the guesswork out, but it also takes away from your personal touch and sometimes your (and your children's) unique personalities. Refer #1 – #3 above.

BLUNDER #5 – Failing to include cross-disciplinary learning

This one is by far the most important, which is why I saved it for last. I have said before that I see homeschooling as a journey not just for the children, but also for the parents. I see homeschooling as a fun, creative, educational pursuit for the entire family. Your goals might be different but they do not mean that you have to be so focused on textbooks and workbooks that you forget curricula that can be had for free!

Don't know what I'm talking about? Read about how Finland recently decided to get rid of individual subjects and teach only through cross-disciplines.

Consider including different media or chucking media altogether and learning through field trips. Think about free classes and other free or inexpensive resources all around you. Engage extended family members, friends, specialists in their fields, go on tours, learn a new craft yourself! Learning is fun. For everyone, regardless of age!

Steer clear of these five most common blunders and have the best homeschool year yet!

Help! I have a skimmer, not a reader!

I'm afraid I have a eight and half year-old speed reader on my hands. In fact, I think he might be worse than a speed reader: he might be a skimmer.

You know the kind – the kind like me. The ones that read the questions first and the comprehension passage later. The ones that instinctively skim the passage because they know all they have to do is answer the questions anyway. No sense getting attached to the characters in the story.

But, wait…

Is that necessarily a bad thing?

When I noticed my son was doing this with his reader, I was troubled. He wasn't doing a careful reading of the passage, I instinctively thought. He needed to read it, understand it and then answer the questions.

He wasn't paying attention the way he was supposed to. He wasn't doing what the workbook was designed for.

But wait, I said. What if he was doing just that – differently?

Kids know how to hack learning and they know it almost as well as we do, perhaps better. Allow me to explain. Think back to the last time you wanted to learn something – say it was a research study on how something affects your body. What did you do?

Did you read the entire study carefully from beginning to end, word by word, or did you quickly look up the one very specific thing you were looking for? Didn't you go back over it only if you needed to? If something didn't make sense or if something seemed odd?

Weren't you then just skimming too?

What I'm trying to get to is that skimming too is a form of reading. It's a form of learning. Not all books need a close, word by word reading. Skimming or speed reading is not something to worry too much about. After all, in the words of Francis Bacon, "Some books are to be tasted, others to be swallowed, and some few to be chewed and digested."

Some books just need to be tasted. In *The first Twenty Hours,* Josh Kaufman emphasizes this. He makes a distinction between acquiring skills and learning. He recommends skimming in the first stage of acquiring skills. This gives you a general sense of where you're going and helps you retain the most important aspects without getting too bogged down by the details, which you probably don't understand yet anyway.

If you are concerned about the reading habits of your child or want him to read deeper, here's a trick: instead of answering the comprehension questions at the bottom of the passage, have him narrate what he just read to you.

But do remember that you might not want to teach skimming out of the child completely. It's a habit that will likely come in handy as he grows.

Skimming is a skill, after all, in focusing on what is most important, ignoring what's not and eliminating distractions.

I feel like I have nothing to show for all the work I do with the children that is not technically curriculum.

Pssst... hey you! Yes, you homeschooling mom! I'm looking at you. Want to know a secret?

You're doing enough.

You're doing more than you think you are.

Don't believe me? Here's a challenge. For the next entire week, write down everything you think your child is learning. If you read to him, write it down. Did you cook or do laundry together? Note it.

Maybe he figured out a map of your neighborhood and told you where to turn the car. If you read a book together or just listened to an audiobook, remember to include it.

Great conversations or any teachable moment you have spent, even the difficult ones - write them down.

Oh, and of course don't forget the overt sit down work you do with your child. All the written work, all the hear-tearing math, everything that required pens and paper and the ubiquitous worksheet.

And then, only then - add it up.

See, you're teaching enough - you're doing far more than you think.

Schools rest on the idea that information can be institutionalized and they have control over all of it. And to get that coveted information, we have to be enrolled in a formal course.

But of course, today we know this is just not true. Teaching isn't something you switch on or off. You don't go from being a mother to a teacher back to being a mother. And that's precisely the point.

Your work as a homeschooler is specialized in the best way possible - it's unique to you and your child.

It doesn't matter if you're still learning patience. Or organization, or frugality, or whatever virtue you think you need to do this successfully. It doesn't matter that inside you feel like you're not doing enough.

It doesn't matter that you're not teaching like a school would.

The fact that you cannot teach like a school - far from being a weakness - is a strength of unfathomable depth.

You are already teaching. You are always teaching. Homeschooling is just another word for it.

I'm not consistent! Will I ever be able to homeschool?

Consistency gurus always get me down. That is when they're not making me feel like an automaton.

"Wake up early every day." "Work out / meditate / read / write first thing in the morning." Continue for forty years.

If that is the measure of success, I'm afraid I'll never reach it. Life just isn't that consistent.

I realized the idea of daily consistency was insane when I came to the conclusion that, as a family, we tend to eat way more on the weekends. We also tend to be out of the home visiting friends or doing things on the weekends as well. And no one (least of all, me!) wants to cook.

So I designated a day late in the week as a big cooking day. We do no school on that day. We pretty much do nothing else except cooking and laundry.

This one day makes our week look ridiculously lopsided. But it's the only way our life works smoothly.

Scheduling is still a good idea if it works. I write much about scheduling and using a template to organize your homeschool and overall it is a good idea to have a vision. But trying to stick to daily consistency is a recipe to make yourself feel guilty and burnt out in no time.

Nothing, but nothing in nature is that consistent. (Okay, yes, the sunrise. But I'm not the sun.) Or we'd all still be mowing our lawns in the winter. So why do we insist on it from our schedules?

Instead, find out if you're one of those people who thrives on a routine and how best to work with your personality. Take the time to find out your children's personalities. And then craft the ideal homeschool. If you're interested in more details on that, I recommend my book *Create Your Own Homeschool Curriculum* on Amazon.

Unless you want to buy into that waking up at five a.m. to work out for forty years advice. In that case, rinse and repeat.

Why wait? I want to get started homeschooling my three-year-old. What would it hurt anyway?

"Do I have to do this?" my son pipes up from his room as he does his sit-down work.

"Do I have to do this part, too?" my daughter echoes from her room after I tell my son that yes, when I assign something, I expect it to be done.

Our homeschool is still smarting from some of my early mistakes. Mea culpa.

You see, we started homeschooling when my daughter was three. Nothing huge, I will add. It was just simple stuff like cutting paper, sticking things, crafts, singing – things like that.

At the time, I was excited about homeschooling and wanting to put some structure on my day with a toddler. I thought it would help us (ahem… me!) as she got older. And then her brother came along and saw what she was doing and he got involved as well. Early.

So here we are with him at age 7 doing multiple digit multiplication and reading well above his grade level.

All well and good, right? Weeeellll, sort of.

The problem is that because I started them early and because I knew that sometimes workbooks and curricula push things that children are not physiologically ready for, I would remove chunks out of whatever book we were using with the words, "Don't do this. You're not ready for it yet."

Sure, we would go back to it later, but not always from the same workbook. I am endlessly eclectic in my choices. It does not bother me to leave a workbook halfway done if the concept has been internalized. But here's the thing: the children got the message that they didn't need to do it if they couldn't.

While I was trying not to overwhelm them with things that were beyond their physiological capabilities, I inadvertently taught them not to apply their abilities at all. Yikes!

This mistake could easily have been avoided with some patience. I could have delayed academic learning.

Instead of rushing on ahead, I could have waited a few more years to get started. Sometimes, just because they can do something, it doesn't mean they should.

Well, lesson learned, people!

My current four-year-old does (almost) no formal learning, even though my daughter loves to play "homeschooling mom" with him. This time, I'll be patient and push only when necessary – much, much later.

Of course, all is not lost and it is possible to break bad habits and learn good ones. But I've had to be intentional about it. And in the interim, I've had to hear some grumbling and groaning – some of it my own.

I am not creative. Can I still homeschool?

Being constantly creative can get exhausting.

One of the pitfalls of classical unschooling is that the planning aspect can take a lot out of the parent.

We want to do right by the kids, so we already tend to take on the full weight of their education. And because we are not interested in following traditional methods, we try to make every single thing interesting.

This is most common in the early years of homeschooling. And this is a mistake.

In my book *Create Your Own Homeschooling Curriculum*, I mention how you should set aside some time before you start homeschooling to observe. This is the time to consider your own preferences and those of your children. This is time to be set aside for deschooling and is not to be part of the regular homeschooling days.

The reason this is done before is so that you are not inclined to second guess yourself throughout the school year every two weeks. Believe me, I've done it.

Sometimes, it's not the curriculum that's the problem. Boredom cannot always be fixed by the homeschooling parent trying a million different ways to make it interesting or creative. Nor should you try.

With apologies to Freud, sometimes a math problem is just a math problem.

Treat it as such, help and guide your child with it. Just as you don't try to make every moment a learning opportunity, just as you don't require a book report on every book read, don't try to make every aspect of education fun.

Not everything needs to be creative and brilliant to be good. Sometimes, work is simply work. And that is just fine.

My children are not as excited about homeschooling as I am. I'm having trouble getting them motivated. What's going on?

I am always the one more visibly excited than my children at the beginning of a new schedule. I have mentioned in my blog that I write out our schedule for 6 – 8 weeks at a time.

As a lover of organization and learning, this is usually the highlight of my day. I look forward fondly to this time every two months or so.

My kids? Not so much.

They like learning – don't doubt that. Especially since I take their specific styles and interests into consideration when I create the curriculum.

But their behavior when I tell them what we will be working on is far from expected. Picture it if you will: here I am, excited, looking forward to getting started and them, lolling about, complaining that "It's going to be too much work."

It's enough for me to label them lazy. It's enough to make me angry, to make me feel like I've been insulted.

Until I realize this: they're not being lazy. They're feeling overwhelmed.

Overwhelmed children do not look like overwhelmed adults.

I have often noted this while doing math with them. When they don't get the concept, they will often twist in their seat and bodily act out what they're feeling in their mind. The discomfort they show will be physical.

My six-year-old son who is learning to read – when he can't sound out a word – will actually laugh hysterically.

If I hadn't seen this often, I would have pegged it for laziness, or worse, goofing off.

"Pay attention!" I would admonish him.

But I am beginning to understand it for what it is. It is not an attack on me or my teaching. It is simply their trepidation at the beginning of something new.

They will grow into it, no doubt.

But at the moment, all they are is overwhelmed. And this is what it looks like.

My child does not enjoy competition and tends to be more of a worrier – just like me. What do I do?

Worry is ubiquitous. It is also entirely normal and can sometimes be helpful. In other words, it's okay to worry.

According to writers Bronson and Merriman, the world is divided into two types of people. There are worriers and then there are warriors.

Some of us enjoy competition, like taking risks and perform better when challenged. These are the warriors.

People who worry, on the other hand, tend to perform worse when circumstances require them to compete against each other or even themselves.

They don't like challenges and prefer to remain in the safe, solid areas of existence.

By now, you already know which category you fall into. So in the interest of full disclosure, I will say that I tend to be a worrier.

Now that the bad news is out of the way, here's the good news: because worriers tend to be focused on small details and anything that can go wrong, they have an advantage that warriors miss.

But this advantage only comes to play when the challenge is repeated more than once.

This means that if you tend to be more of a worrier than a warrior, you are likely to hang back a little and watch. While watching, you notice the things that could be hazards. You try, you fail. You try again, you fail again.

Here's the thing: each time you try and fail, you literally fail better.

What does this have to do with homeschooling? Quite a bit, actually. If you are a worrier, now you know what to do. You can do something enough times in order to succeed.

If your child is a warrior, give him some competition and watch him blossom. If he's a worrier, give him measured challenges and make them repetitive.

Worriers and warriors can both win - just in vastly different ways.

How do I find time for selfcare as a homeschooling mom who spends all day with the children?

"I know it's you who comes home from work," I say to my husband after a particularly long day in a weeklong winter string of long days. "But I feel like it's me."

It hadn't been until I said that out loud that I realized how true it was. Staying home with three children, effectively and attentively (read patiently!) teaching them to read and do fractions is work. Planning meals, budgeting and making sure everyone has clean underwear is labor.

I show up every single day. Most days, I don't punch out until my husband comes home. Long days for him mean longer days for me. A week of this and I'm exhausted.

Depleted.

So what does self-care look like for someone like me?

I will admit, in the past, it has been easy for me to say things like, "Take the day off!" It has worked. And it still works on some days. There is a certain beauty in knowing when to roll up a school day and toss it in the veritable basket of bad lesson plans and unused curricula.

But there is a limit to how many days can be tossed aside. Eventually, my school conscience shows up, dressed in pink and clears her throat.

"If you only do things when you feel like doing them…" she begins, channeling Professor Umbridge. I quickly acquiesce, at the slightest hint of another personal rule. I really, really don't need another rule. But I really, really like making them when any seeming chaos shows up in my day.

So for someone like me who is an eclectic classical unschooler with occasional (especially monthly) bouts of anxiety and depression, what is a workable model of self care?

It has been a while since I read it, but an idea from Jordan Peterson's *12 Rules for Life* has stuck with me. It occurred to me as I was mulling over this concern.

The idea is simply this: to make a deal with yourself and then to keep it.

Making a deal is easy. Work with me on this one, you tell yourself, and then I'll do something nice for you, something you like.

To be fair, I've made a myriad deals like that. But keeping them is a completely different animal. But because I let myself down on a regular basis, the repetitive failure makes me distrust myself and refuse to do things I really want to do.

I mention this to my husband and he, who is currently reading the book, quips, "Oh yeah, that's the rule of treating yourself as someone you are responsible for helping."

Now, I will admit, when he said that, I imagined a nurse. And just the mere fact of that image and what that meant made me anxious. I can barely keep up with my current life, I thought. Now I'm supposed to act like I'm a nurse?

But then it struck me. Wait a minute, I thought. What if it was my daughter in my place? What would I rather have her do? What advice would I give her? This was easier for me to imagine.

I would tell her, I knew then, that she could get schoolwork done in a comfortable environment with attention and focus and then reward herself in the afternoon with something she enjoyed doing that did not demand much from her.

As a parenthesis, that last part is equally important as the rest. So go read it again. If you have anxiety, even calling a babysitter can seem like too much planning. But you can try and give yourself a reward that doesn't require too much from you. Planning a big reward like a day out, date night or the equivalent can drain me in itself, so it's important to remember to plan a recompense that is fairly undemanding.

Framed in this way, the question answered itself.

Even on rough emotional days, I would navigate the choppy waters if only to get to the perfect calm of the afternoon. I would plan a reward and follow through on it. I would gain back trust in myself and thus could pave the way slowly to working through difficult days.

This is what self-care looks like for me currently. It seems like an oversimplification, but there is wisdom here, especially on days that you just can't take off, especially if you tend to be a little existentialist like me and feel the weight of finishing a day with nothing done.

Because, sometimes, self-care has to include getting stuff done.

What about the gaps in learning my children will have? How can I be sure to cover all the bases of their education?

Every single time I attend a homeschooling conference, there is an inevitable question that gets asked by new homeschoolers.

"But what about the gaps in learning?"

It's a normal concern, I suppose. And anything is better than the socialization question that plagues new homeschoolers, but the gaps question is also an age-old one and needs to be addressed.

I have gaps in learning as well. I was recently watching *Penny Dreadful* with my husband. And I realized that I had never read *Frankenstein*. Not a big deal, I know.

But I am a literature major. And a writing major. How was it that I had made it through college and written so much about it and yet never read it? I had to fix the problem immediately, I decided. I downloaded my free copy and began reading it on my Kindle immediately.

It's a small example, I know. But a significant one. Sometimes, information seems to permeate around us so much, we know enough about it but don't know it.

Everyone has gaps in learning!

The fear most would be homeschoolers have when they begin is that they will somehow leave out something important. They are afraid of failing their children. And noble as this concern is, it is unfounded.

There is no mastermind in public schools that ensures there will not be gaps.

Everyone has gaps - this is the nature of education. Especially self-directed education.

Think about all the things you looked up this week - recipes, lyrics of songs, instructions on how to put something together, plans, meanings of words, maps, even perhaps names of people you thought you knew. These were gaps in your learning. And you knew how to fix them.

If the Age of Information has taught us anything, it is this: gaps are inevitable. And that's another nail in the coffin of public school. And for that, I welcome the realization.

A sacrosanct tome of information downloaded into your brain has always been a myth, but that myth was at no time more obvious than it is today.

Our Homeschool is not a Well-Oiled Machine and Never Will Be

When I first became a stay at home mom, I thought about things like efficiency. I wanted everything to be streamlined so it could get done. We liked saving time. We loved saving money. I wanted to run my home and by extension our homeschool like a well-oiled machine.

It has taken me almost a decade to realize what an impossibility that is.

The problem, I have realized, about trying to run a home, a family or an education like a well-oiled machine is that it is made up of people. And to make it even harder, it is made of people who are still trying on new roles.

There are the children, yes, that everyone will tell you "are preparing for the future" and it's "your duty to raise them right." It's their first time, they will tell you, it's their first time being a tween, being a teenager, being a baby, a child. But surely, you know? You know how hard it is and you have been that age. And now you're an adult. You know.

Don't you?

Here's the problem, though: it's my first time, too.

It's my first time being a mother and a wife. It's my first time being a mother to a tween. It's my first time having three children at the grocery store, my first time buying

Christmas presents for everyone, first time planning meals and sticking to a budget, first time trying to potty train.

It's my first time, too.

And so, no. I don't know. I don't know what it is like to comfort a six-year-old who is distraught that the older two children seem to be bullying him. I don't know what's going through their minds as they try to tell him they weren't trying to be mean, they were just playing, remember?

I'm an adult, but I have never been through this specific thing before. This thing, this very important thing staring me in the face right now that demands I pay attention to it, resolve it.

I just don't know.

To plan perfectly, to have everything move along in a streamlined, beautiful, orchestrated manner, to have our homeschool work like a well-oiled machine, I would need everything behave in the same way day in and day out.

To make running my home and homeschool like a well-oiled machine, I would need everyone including myself to be a cog. Worse, I would need everyone to practice being a cog.

There would be no surprises and everything would move along smoothly because every day would be the same. The children would look to me for advice on what to do and I would dispense it with a beatific smile on my face.

No, thank you.

I know. We're a mess. And it's perfect. And I intend to keep it this way as long as I can.

Acknowledgments

Thank you to all my readers and fellow homeschoolers. Your feedback, friendship and support has kept me writing and sharing pieces of my life and turned the difficult homeschooling days into fodder.

Thank you to my children, willing (and sometimes unwilling) subjects in our educational experiments.

And, as always, a huge thank you to my husband, who knows I am far from perfect and loves me anyway.

Copyright © 2019 Purva Brown

All rights reserved. This book or any portion thereof may not be reproduced or used in any manner whatsoever without the express written permission of the author except for the use of brief quotations.

Cover photo by Fabrizio Verrecchia on Unsplash

Made in the USA
San Bernardino, CA
14 May 2019